Healthful Indian Flavors with *Alamelu*

Also by Alamelu Vairavan

Healthy South Indian Cooking

Indian Inspired Gluten-Free Cooking

Healthful Indian Flavors with Alamelu

Alamelu Vairavan

Photography by Linda Smallpage

Hippocrene Books, Inc.
New York

*This cookbook is related to the Milwaukee Public Television show
"Healthful Indian Flavors with Alamelu."*

For further information, contact:
HIPPOCRENE BOOKS, INC.
171 Madison Avenue
New York, NY 10016
www.hippocrenebooks.com

Library of Congress Cataloging-in-Publication Data

Names: Vairavan, Alamelu, author.
Title: Healthful Indian flavors with Alamelu / Alamelu Vairavan ;
    photographs by Linda Smallpage.
Description: New York : Hippocrene Books, Inc., [2016] |
Contains the recipes featured on the first three seasons of Alamelu Vairavan's popular
MPTV/PBS cooking series. | Includes index.
Identifiers: LCCN 2016034691| ISBN 9780781813587 (paperback) |
    ISBN 0781813581 (paperback)
Subjects: LCSH: Cooking, India. | Health. | LCGFT: Cookbooks.
Classification: LCC TX724 .V3323 2016 | DDC 641.5954--dc23
    LC record available at https://lccn.loc.gov/2016034691

DEDICATION

I dedicate this book to my loving family
and to the numerous people who have encouraged me
in my culinary journey

CONTENTS

Foreword by Dr. Bharat Aggarwal   ix
Introduction: My Inspiring Culinary Journey   1
Spices & Other Basic Ingredients   3
Shopping List for Spices and Other Basics   10
Glossary of South Indian Dishes   12
General Cooking Tips   14

RECIPE CHAPTERS

Appetizers   17
Chutneys & Sauces   35
Soups   49
Breakfast   59
Rice & Quinoa   77
Salads   105
Sambhars & Kulambus   115
Vegetable Dishes   141
Non-Vegetarian Dishes   223
Desserts   259

Suggested Menus   265
Fusion Thanksgiving Menu & Recipes   267
Index   269
Acknowledgments   275
About the Author   276

Foreword

Almost twenty-five centuries ago, the ancient Greek physician Hippocrates advised, "Let food be thy medicine and medicine be thy food." Nowadays we have paraphrased his idea in slogans like "You Are What You Eat." In more recent history, nearly five centuries ago, Vasco da Gama and Christopher Columbus, despite hardship, danger, and deprivation at sea, were drawn on by the powerful lure of spices, one of the most valuable commodities in the Old World. We all know that spices greatly enhance the flavor of food, but they have also been credited with preserving food and improving its medicinal value. Because most spices are powerful antioxidants, they not only serve as food-preservatives but they also preserve our bodies once we ingest them. My book, *Healing Spices: How to Use 50 Everyday and Exotic Spices to Boost Health and Beat Disease* (Sterling) covers the healing properties of commonly used herbs and spices.

In *Healthful Indian Flavors with Alamelu*, Alamelu Vairavan artfully combines spices, herbs, and healthful ingredients in recipes that are highly palliative, highly delicious, and highly medicinal. If you want to learn how to make flavorful appetizers, soups, chutneys, vegetarian and non-vegetarian dishes, dals (lentils), and desserts, this book provides excellent and systematic recipes for a variety of wholesome dishes. Alamelu is a skilled and knowledgeable guide, showing readers how to prepare tasty, nutritious meals. She provides multiple ways to prepare rice and vegetables—both heart-healthy staples in the diets of many global communities.

In our research on the links between diet and health, my colleagues and I have documented pulses, and over a dozen varieties of cereals and nuts and their health benefits.* Alamelu's recipes make use of a remarkable variety of vegetables, ensuring that readers and home cooks can choose from a diverse range of healthful options. She also introduces readers to the assortment of protein-rich dals (legumes) that are common in Indian cooking. These make an excellent and heart-healthy vegetarian options to meat. After all, as another saying goes, "Variety is the Spice of Life."

To return to the all-important subject of spices—so many spices used in Indian cooking are valued for their antioxidant and anti-inflammatory properties. One in particular, however, bright yellow turmeric (known in Hindi as *haldi*), is among the most revered and beneficial of Indian spices. Over nine thousand scientific reports have been published on turmeric alone, and it has been extolled in both the centuries-old Ayurvedic tradition and in modern practice. Readers will be pleased to see turmeric is a key ingredient in many of Alamelu's recipes.

I highly recommend *Healthful Indian Flavors with Alamelu* to readers who want to take advantage of the powerful, healing antioxidant qualities of spices and at the same time, indulge in the flavor-rich, wholesome offerings of Indian cuisine.

Dr. Bharat Aggarwal
Founding Director, Inflammation Research Institute, San Diego, California
Former Professor of Experimental Therapeutics, Cancer Medicine and Immunology,
The University of Texas M. D. Anderson Cancer Center, Houston, Texas

---

*Bharat B. Aggarwal and Sunil Krishnan and Sushovan Guha, eds. *Inflammation, Lifestyle and Chronic Diseases: The Silent Link.* New York: CRC Press, 2011.

Introduction:
My Inspiring Culinary Journey

My culinary journey has been both remarkable and rewarding. It began when I arrived in the United States from India as a young bride. Although I knew absolutely nothing about cooking itself, I did enjoy good food. I grew up in India in a loving family that employed a full-time cook who created fabulous foods everyday. I also had the luxury of eating delicious foods at the hospitable homes of many relatives. There was neither a need nor an opportunity for me to step into the kitchen. Starting married life in America changed all that!

Fortunately, I was able to learn cooking with lessons from a great Indian chef, Chettinad Natesan, then employed at my aunt Visalakshi Alagappan's home in Queens, New York, where I stayed for several weeks while my husband completed his doctoral studies at the University of Notre Dame. Then, over the years, I continued to learn authentic as well as new Indian cooking techniques during regular visits to India.

While comfortably feeding my husband and two children, I also enjoyed entertaining friends and neighbors in Whitefish Bay, Wisconsin, where we raised our family. Soon I became confident enough to give cooking demonstrations in local schools and other public places. My neighbor and dear friend Dr. Patricia Marquardt showed great interest in learning from me, and our joint cooking sessions led to our first cookbook, *The Art of South Indian Cooking* (Hippocrene Books, 1997). That was an early breakthrough in my culinary journey.

Soon after, I was invited to appear on a national television program, "Home Matters" on the Discovery Channel. I was thrilled to learn that my premier television appearance was on a show that also featured the great American chef Julia Child who preceded me in the same segment. The omen was great, and I sensed good things would follow! Indeed more books and television guest appearances did. One thing, as we know, leads to another. I was happy to give various culinary presentations at food-related events, including the famous Kohler Food and Wine Festival in Wisconsin, where a wine expert discussed appropriate wines to go with the foods I had cooked. An unforgettable experience during my culinary journey was a sold-out workshop entitled "Enticing Indian Flavors" that I presented at the James Beard Foundation in New York in 2009.

Cooking classes with small and large groups, and culinary presentations at libraries, hospitals, and university outreach programs, and even book-signing events, gave me great pleasure because I met many interesting people eager to learn healthful cooking. Sharing my knowledge of healthy Indian cooking was very rewarding.

During the early part of my culinary journey, I also worked full-time as a manager of health information systems in a long-term care nursing facility. I am grateful to my husband, K.V., my son Ashok, my daughter Valli, and my friend Pat for their invaluable support and encouragement during those years. As I progressed in my journey I realized the intense interest I had developed for my culinary activities and decided to change careers. I quit my job so that I could spend more time pursuing my culinary passion.

Two significant developments reinforced my new found career. First, the publication of my recipes in a book by the American Dietetic Association titled *Cooking Healthy Across America* (John Wiley Publishers, 2005); and second, a similar inclusion of some of my recipes in *Healing Spices: How to use everyday and exotic spices to boost health and beat disease*, a book by Dr. Bharat Aggarwal, then with M.D. Anderson Cancer Center, and Debra Yost (Sterling Publishing Company, 2011).

Around the same time, I reached an important milestone in my journey. Milwaukee Public Television (MPTV) produced a culinary series with me as the host. The series, "Healthful Indian Flavors with Alamelu," was originally shown in Wisconsin beginning in 2011 and subsequently broadcast by PBS around the country. More seasons of the TV series followed. PBS CREATE aired episodes from the new seasons nationally. I am grateful to MPTV and PBS for this opportunity to spread the word about healthful cooking not only in Wisconsin but also around the country. I cannot find adequate words to express my gratitude to the numerous viewers from all over America who took the time to let me know how much they enjoyed and benefited from the shows. When I started recording the shows, I had no idea that so many people would find them enjoyable and helpful. For example, how can anyone not be inspired or fulfilled by viewer comments such as the following?:

"We watch you on KLRU in Austin (Texas), and enjoy the simpleness of your cooking. My husband had to completely change his diet due to some heart trouble a few years ago, and we are always looking for good food that's easy to prepare. And you deliver!"

"What an inspiration you are! Now I have been able to cook and enjoy authentic Indian cuisine in my home. I adore all your shows and healthful tips. Thank you so much for you and all you do; it has transformed my kitchen and the aromas are heaven sent!"

Indeed the inspiration to write this book came from encouraging comments from television viewers. Many of them went on to ask for a companion cookbook for the television shows. This cookbook is intended partially to meet such requests, but it is important to note that the book can be used independently of the shows. In writing this cookbook I have benefited from valuable comments from television viewers and users of my previous cookbooks, *Healthy South Indian Cooking* (Hippocrene Books) and *Indian Inspired Gluten-Free Cooking* (Hippocrene Books). This new cookbook includes improved versions of select recipes from the earlier cookbooks, as well as new recipes.

Sharing my culinary passion with others has been one of the most rewarding experiences of my life. I have discovered cooking is a skill worth learning. It is my hope that this book will not only be helpful to current cooks and aspiring chefs but also to future generations like my young twin grandsons Surav and Mihir and help them discover the joy and benefits of healthful cooking.

As you embark on your own culinary journey using this book as a guide, I hope you also will discover the joy of cooking and enjoying healthful foods with enticing Indian flavors.

Spices and Other Basic Ingredients

SPICES AND SPICE BLENDS

Asafoetida: A strongly scented resin used in small quantities in some vegetable and rice dishes, it imparts a flavor reminiscent of onion and garlic. Asafoetida is sold in lump or powdered form. The powdered form (ground) is available in Indian grocery stores.

Bay Leaves: Long, dried green leaves that add a subtle flavor to any dish. Bay leaves have a sweet, woody aroma much like that of cinnamon and a slightly pungent flavor. They are added to warm oil to enhance the flavor of rice and meat dishes and can be removed from a dish before serving.

Black Mustard Seeds: Small, round, black seeds, raw mustard seeds have almost no smell, but on cooking they impart an earthy, nutty aroma. When mustard seeds are dropped in a small amount of hot oil, they pop and crackle as they give out a distinctive flavor. Black mustard seeds (also known as brown mustard seeds) are available in spice stores, regular grocery stores, and Indian grocery stores. If you can't find black mustard seeds you may use yellow mustard seeds.

Black Peppercorns: Black pepper is known as the "king of all spices." Black peppercorns add a great amount of flavor to many dishes. Pepper was valued as much as gold in the thirteenth century. Today pepper is freely available around the world and is used in almost every cuisine. The taste of pepper is just spicy hot and its aroma is pungent. It is known as an appetite stimulant and as a digestive spice.

A WORD ABOUT USING SPICES AND CHILIES

Spices have intrinsic health benefits. There is growing evidence that because of their antioxidant and anti-inflammatory properties spices like turmeric have a healing power in treating or preventing many diseases. Spices also add flavor to foods, reducing a need for salt.

Some people may be reluctant to try recipes with spices fearing that they do not enjoy hot and spicy foods. But rest assured that the recipes in this book do not have to be too spicy or hot. The hotness of a dish comes mostly from chilies or cayenne pepper powder. You can use chilies and cayenne in small quantities (as presented in the recipes here) in such a way that they do not overwhelm the vegetables, but add subtle flavors and aromas to the dishes. Vegetable and rice dishes come alive when enhanced by spices and herbs. The result can be tasty and aromatic foods that are hard to resist. You can transform even broccoli, Brussels sprouts, spinach, cabbage, and lima beans into dishes that are tasty and visually appealing. You may be amazed how even vegetable haters can be transformed into vegetable lovers when spices and legumes are used in cooking.

Besides giving foods a "kick", chilies have nutritional values. For instance, ounce for ounce, green chili peppers have twice as much vitamin C as an orange and contain more vitamin C than a carrot. Chili peppers increase circulation and can warm you up on a cold day. Studies have shown that chili peppers do not aggravate, and may even help those with ulcers and gastrointestinal problems. Eating chili peppers is a good way to curb appetite and control cravings. The compound "capsaicin" found in chili peppers is anti-inflammatory and has antioxidant properties.

Black Pepper and Cumin Powder: Grinding equal parts peppercorns and cumin seeds together into a fine powder makes an aromatic spice blend (no need to roast before grinding). In my opinion, it is also a great salt substitute! Delicious when used over fried eggs and also in flavored rice and vegetable dishes. Either grind them together yourself or ground black pepper and ground cumin are sold separately in grocery and spice stores. Simply mix half and half and keep in a jar on your shelf to use as needed.

Cardamom: Cardamom is a pod consisting of an outer shell with little flavor and tiny inner seeds with intense flavor. Ground cardamom has an intensely strong flavor and is easy to use. Cardamom is known as the "queen of all spices." Ground cardamom is used to flavor rice and meat dishes and also in spiced Chai tea.

Cayenne Pepper Powder (Red Pepper Powder): Cayenne pepper powder has the power to make any dish fiery hot, but it also has a subtle flavor-enhancing quality. Cayenne pepper powder mixed with ground cumin adds an amazing flavor to dishes. Usually used in small amounts, the hotness of a dish can be controlled by the amount of cayenne pepper powder used.

Chutney Powder: An aromatic blend of spices including coriander seeds, red chili peppers, curry leaves, asafoetida, and toovar dal. Chutney powder comes prepackaged and I recommend the MTR brand that is available in Indian grocery stores and also on Amazon.

Cinnamon Sticks: The aromatic, reddish-brown bark of the cinnamon tree imparts a rich, sweet flavor to foods. Cinnamon sticks are sometimes cracked down to small slivers to be used in cooking. The taste is warm, sharply sweet, and aromatic. Cinnamon and bay leaf cooked together enhances the flavor of vegetable, meat, and rice dishes. Cinnamon sticks can be removed before serving. Ground cinnamon can also be used in place of cinnamon sticks (¼ to ½ teaspoon of ground cinnamon per stick). Add ground cinnamon when adding other ground spices to a dish.

Cloves: Whole cloves are used for flavoring sauces and stocks. The flavor is intense, so be sure to use sparingly. Ground cloves are perfect for flavored rice dishes.

Coriander: Coriander seeds have a light, lemony flavor that combines well with other spices. Ground coriander is prepared by roasting and grinding the seeds. The leaves of the coriander plant are called cilantro in the U.S.

Cumin Seeds: Cumin is appreciated for both its aroma and medicinal qualities. The small, oblong, brown seeds resemble caraway seeds and have a peppery flavor. Cumin is an essential ingredient in curry powder and garam masala powder. When cumin seeds are dry-roasted or added to warm oil, they impart a rich aroma that enhances rice or vegetable dishes. **Ground Cumin (Cumin Powder):** Ground cumin blends well with many spices. Ground cumin blended with cayenne pepper powder or with ground black pepper lends distinctive flavor to any dish. (See Black Pepper and Cumin Powder above.)

Curry Powder: A blend of many spices such as coriander, fenugreek, cumin, black pepper, red chili pepper, and turmeric. Commercial blends of curry powder are readily available in regular grocery stores. Curry powders are used in chicken, fish, and shrimp dishes. It is available in two varieties: sweet curry powder (not too spicy) and hot curry powder (more hot pepper and ginger)—choose according to your taste.

Fennel Seeds: Fennel seeds are a much-used spice in India. A vibrant green, the seeds have a warm, sweet, and intense licorice flavor that turns mild on roasting. Fennel seeds are a powerful antioxidant and anti-inflammatory.

Fenugreek Seeds: Small, hard, oblong brown seeds, fenugreek seeds are slightly bitter in taste. Roasting the seeds subdues the flavor. It is an important spice ingredient in curry powder.

Garam Masala: The heart of most North Indian dishes, garam masala is a blending of several dry-roasted and ground spices. "*Masala*" refers to a combination of several spices and "*garam*" means spice intensity referring to spice richness. Garam masala powder is usually a combination of spices such as coriander seeds, cumin seeds, cardamom, black peppercorns, cloves, cinnamon, and bay leaves.

Rasam Powder: An aromatic blend of many spices including coriander seeds, red chili peppers, cumin seeds, curry leaves, and asafoetida. Rasam powder comes prepackaged and I recommend the MTR brand that is available in Indian grocery stores and also on Amazon.

Sambhar Powder: An aromatic blend of spices and dals including red chili peppers, cumin seeds, curry leaves, fenugreek seeds, asafoetida, chana dal, and toovar dal. Sambhar powder is readily available packaged as "Madras Sambhar powder" (MTR brand) in Indian grocery stores and also on Amazon.

Turmeric (Ground/Powder): One of the great Indian spices and known as Indian gold, ground turmeric is a yellow root that has been dried and powdered and imparts a musty flavor and bright yellow color to any dish. Turmeric contains the compound curcumin and is recognized by many as an antioxidant, anti-cancer, and anti-inflammatory substance. Growing research suggests that turmeric may help prevent arthritis and a host of other diseases including Alzheimers. Lately turmeric is becoming increasingly popular with scientists and physicians who are embracing the natural benefits it provides.

GRAINS AND DALS

Rice: Rice is one of the most versatile grains. Rice is served plain with saucy dishes, and tossed with vegetables, legumes, and meat, and used in desserts. Rice pilafs are well-known in Indian, Chinese, and Middle Eastern cuisines. In India, there are a variety of flavored rice dishes and it is a staple comfort food.

Basmati Rice: an aromatic, creamy white or hardy brown long-grain rice grown in the Himalayan foothills of India and in California, basmati rice is a fragrant, high-quality rice. This rice is preferred for making both plain and flavored rice dishes. It has a nutty flavor and comes packaged under several brand names. The grains of rice are finer than the grains of other types of rice, and they separate beautifully after they are cooked. Basmati rice is unexcelled in making pilafs and flavored rice dishes. When purchasing basmati rice, look for a quality brand, such as Dehradun or Tilda, available in natural food stores and Indian grocery stores.

Brown Rice: more nutritious than polished white rice, brown rice supplies more fiber. When cooked, the plump, rounded kernels of short- and medium-grain brown rice are soft, moist, and slightly sticky. Although white and basmati rice are commonly used in Indian cooking, you may also prepare the recipes with brown rice. You may find that the nutty flavor and high fiber content of the brown rice compensates for its lack of lightness and delicacy.

Extra-Long-Grain Rice: used in making plain and flavored rice dishes, this rice lacks the aromatic quality of basmati or jasmine rice, but it is a good all-purpose rice. It is available in regular supermarkets.

Jasmine Rice: a delicate and aromatic pure white rice. It is excellent for making plain or flavored rice dishes. It is available in Indian and Asian grocery stores.

Quinoa (*pronounced keen-wa*): Hardy and nutritious with a unique texture and taste, quinoa is a gluten-free complete protein source. It is a member of the same food family as spinach, Swiss chard, and beets. Quinoa comes in many colors, including tan, red, orange, pink, purple, and black.

Dals (Lentils): Legumes that are high in protein and fiber, dals are a staple ingredient in many Indian dishes. There are numerous varieties of dals, but in the recipes in this cookbook, I use either Masoor Dal (Red Lentils), Moong Dal (Mung Lentils), or Yellow Split Peas. Urad dal is used as a seasoning lentil for many vegetable dishes and also used with rice to make breakfast dishes like idlis, dosais, etc.

Masoor Dal (Red Lentils): An orange-red colored lentil, also known as red lentil, in split form it is used in making saucy dishes. Masoor dal cooks fast and takes only 15 to 20 minutes! Masoor dal can be substituted for toor dal in *sambhars* and other vegetable dishes. These red lentils make tasty soups and vegetable dishes and saucy dishes without the use of heavy cream. Masoor dal is available in natural food stores and Indian grocery stores.

Moong Dal (Yellow Mung Beans / Yellow Lentils): A golden yellow lentil used in split form, this most versatile of dals cooks quickly and is widely used in making vegetarian dishes.

Toor Dal or Toovar Dal: A kind of yellow lentil that is split into two round halves. Toor dal takes time to cook and is traditionally cooked to a creamy consistency to make sambhars, kootus, and soups. It creates the rich base so characteristic of delicious sambhars. Toor dal is available in Indian grocery stores.

Urad Dal: A creamy white split lentil. Urad dal sautéed in oil lends a nutty, crunchy taste to dishes. Essential to South Indian cooking, urad dal is used both as a seasoning and as a base for *vadas, idlis,* and *dosais*. Urad dal, enhanced with black mustard seeds and various seasonings, is an essential ingredient in many recipes. When whole, urad dal has a black skin and is known as black gram lentil. The recipes in this book use the split, cream-colored urad dal exclusively, available in Indian grocery stores and on Amazon.

Yellow Split Peas: A familiar kind of legume, readily available in regular grocery stores, yellow split peas have a distinctive texture and taste. Yellow split peas cook quickly in about thirty minutes. When yellow split peas are cooked, they look like corn and have a mild flavor. When cooked split peas are added to vegetable dishes they add taste and color to the dish. Yellow split peas are used to make dishes such as *vadas, podimas, pachadis,* and *kootus*.

OTHER INGREDIENTS

Chili Garlic Sauce: Readily available in regular grocery stores, chili-garlic sauce adds zest to chicken and fish dishes.

Cilantro / Coriander: A distinctively aromatic herb of major importance in Indian cuisine, cilantro may be purchased as fresh cilantro leaves, coriander seeds, or in its dried form as ground coriander. Cilantro is used both as a garnish and for making chutneys.

Coconut: The edible inner flesh is widely used as a garnish for cooked vegetables and as a base for chutneys and sauces. Shredded fresh coconut is available in the freezer section of natural and Indian grocery stores. Unsweetened coconut powder is also available in natural food stores. The coconut water inside the coconut shell supports rapid hydration. Coconut water is all natural and has the nutrition needed to hydrate the body. Coconut milk is different from coconut water as it is the creamy milk extracted from the coconut meat. It looks like heavy cream and is often used in saucy Thai dishes.

Garlic: A bulbous herb composed of individual cloves this is an essential ingredient in South Indian cooking. Used in most soups, vegetables, and meat dishes to enhance flavor, it is frequently sautéed in hot oil at the outset of a recipe, and infuses the entire dish with a distinctively pleasing flavor. Garlic with ginger makes a delicious combination paste. Great curative powers are attributed to garlic.

Ginger Root: A root spice with a warm, fresh flavor that is used often in Indian cooking both as a fundamental ingredient and as a garnish. Ginger in combination with garlic is very popular and adds wonderful flavor to any dish. Ginger is also available in powdered form, but fresh ginger is highly recommended for its flavor and healthful qualities. It is valued as a medicinal spice also and aids in digestion.

Green Chili Peppers (Serrano, Jalapeno, Thai Chilies): Fresh unripe chili peppers are a common ingredient that impart a spicy, hot flavor to many Indian dishes. There are a wide variety of chili peppers and you may use any of the many types available, depending on the amount of heat you prefer. Chilies are used in virtually every savory dish in India. Chilies may be used sparingly, however, or omitted altogether depending on your taste. In general, the smaller the chili pepper, the hotter it is.

Mint: A fragrant herb with a uniquely fresh flavor and aroma, mint is used in Indian cuisine primarily in cooling chutneys and relishes that balance the more spicy dishes.

Oils: When choosing oil for cooking the dishes in this book it is important to have a high smoke point. Choose any of the following oils you prefer: canola oil, olive oil, extra-light or extra-virgin olive oil, or coconut oil.

Onions: A staple ingredient valued for its flavor and medicinal qualities, onions sautéed in oil with various spices are the foundation of most savory Indian dishes. Onions also appear raw in yogurt salad and as a garnish for other dishes.

Salt: Most salt is highly refined and very white. Some sea salts retain the minerals which appear as small, dark, or colored particles. If you have been advised by your healthcare provider to cut back on sodium then any form of salt should be reduced as the sodium content is the same by weight. Coarse or kosher salt may appear to be lower in sodium because less "fits" in the measuring spoon than if it is finely ground. Reduced sodium salt has a filler added so if you "salt to taste" and add more you can end up with the same amount of sodium. You can adjust the amount of sodium in the recipes to your taste and health needs. With all the other spices in the dishes, most people do not notice a lack of salt.

Tamarind Paste: Beans with a sweet and sour taste, when ground to a paste they add a certain tartness to dishes. Tamarind is known as the "Indian date." Bottled tamarind paste is available in Indian grocery stores. Lemon juice may be substituted.

Tomato sauce: In the recipes in this book I have listed regular canned tomato sauce as this is the easiest to find, but sodium varies for every brand and can be as high as 410 mg. per ¼ cup. I usually choose to use a no-salt-added variety as this gives a better flavor and you have more control over the sodium content of the recipes. You can then choose to leave the added salt out completely to reduce sodium even further or add more as desired. You can also use fresh, plump ripe tomatoes placed in a blender and puréed into a sauce in place of the canned.

Whole Dried Red Chili Peppers: Chilies have a strong, sharp aroma and their taste ranges from mild to dynamite. The level of heat is dependent on the amount of "capsaicin" present in the seeds. Chilies are available fresh, dried, powdered, flaked in oil, and in sauce form, bottled, and pickled. Chilies are high in vitamins A and C and have more vitamin C per gram than an orange! Chili peppers are capsicums, in the same family as bell peppers and paprika pods. Ranging in flavor from rich and sweet to fiery hot, "Sanaam," "Arbol," "Dundicut," "Tien Tsin," and "Cascabel" are all dried hot peppers. When a whole pepper is added to hot oil the flavor of the infused oil gives a very rich, full-bodied taste to dishes. You may remove the whole pepper before serving.

Shopping List for Spices and Other Basics

With very few exceptions, the spices used in Indian cooking can be found in most American supermarkets. Other spices can be bought economically from Indian and Asian grocery stores or from stores specializing in spices. One may also order spices online from many Indian grocery stores or online retailers in the United States and Canada. Once a basic pantry of Indian spices is assembled, you will be able to use them time and again in numerous recipes that often call for the same ingredients in similar order.

Note: Because spices are commonly labeled in Hindi or sometimes Tamil in Indian groceries, I have provided those names for items in parentheses after the English name: *(Hindi / Tamil)*.

SPICES

Asafoetida powder *(Hing / Perungayam)*

Bay leaves *(Tez patta / Lavangilai)*

Black mustard seeds *(Rai / Kadugu)*

Black peppercorns, whole and/or ground *(Kalimirch / Milagu)*

Cayenne pepper powder

Cinnamon *(Dal chini / Pattai)*

Cumin seeds and/or ground cumin *(Jeera / Jeerakam)*

Fennel seeds *(Saunf or Sonf / Perunjeeragam)*

Fenugreek seeds *(Methi / Venthayam)*

Poppy seeds, white *(Kus khus / Kus kus), ground raw almonds can be substituted*

Red chili pepper, whole dried and/or powdered *(Mirch / Milagaai)*

Saffron *(Zaffran or Kesar / Kungumappu)*

Tamarind paste *(Imli / Puli)*

Turmeric, ground/powder *(Haldi / Manjal)*

SPICE BLENDS
(MTR and Deepa brands are recommended)

Ground black pepper & ground cumin blend *(this is not usually found in stores so you will need to combine the two spices in equal portions to make the spice blend and store in a jar to use as needed)*

Chutney powder *(MTR brand)*

Curry powder, hot or medium *(available at Penzeys and Indian groceries)*

STORING SPICES AND DALS

Most spices keep best in sealed glass bottles or containers. Tightly closed, spices will retain their quality for many months and even for a year or two. I highly recommend removing spices, powders, and dals from their plastic wraps and storing them in bottles with identifying labels. Spices kept in the kitchen cupboard in jars will retain flavor, aroma, and color. Dals can be stored in glass or metal containers. There are various size jars available in spice shops and in discount stores.

Garam Masala

Rasam powder *(MTR brand)*

Sambhar powder *(MTR brand)*

RICE & QUINOA

Extra-long-grain rice

Basmati rice, white or brown

Jasmine rice

Brown rice

Quinoa

LENTILS / DALS

Moong dal (Split Yellow Mung Beans / *Paruppu*)

Masoor dal (Red lentils / *Mysoor Paruppu*)

Yellow split peas *(Matar ki dal)*

Urad dal (Black gram dal / *Ulutham Paruppu*), skinned and split

Urad Dal
Black Mustard Seeds
Cumin Seeds

Glossary of South Indian Dishes

Adai
A type of thick, fiber-rich pancake made from a variety of dals. Batter for adais does not require fermentation. Just soak dals, grind coarsely, and make adais immediately.

Biriyani Rice (Pulaoo Rice)
A kind of aromatic fried rice infused with the flavors of cinnamon and clove.

Chutney
A savory sauce used as an accompaniment to appetizers and breakfast items. There are a variety of delicious chutneys featured in this book. Unlike their North Indian counterparts, the South Indian chutneys are not sweet.

Dosai
A South Indian thin pancake or crepe made from ground rice and urad dal that has been allowed to ferment. Dosai is a South Indian breakfast specialty and can be prepared in a variety of ways. One favorite variety is Masala Dosai, which is dosai stuffed with a delicious filling of potato masala and coconut chutney.

Idiyappam
A dish made with steam-cooked thin rice noodles called rice sticks. Packages of dry rice sticks are available in Indian and Oriental stores. Rice sticks are cooked in boiling water like pasta, then are drained and seasoned to make a delicious breakfast or a light supper.

Idli
Delicate steamed rice cake that is a South Indian specialty. Idlis are made from a fermented batter similar to that used to make dosais. Idlis and dosais are popular breakfast foods usually served with sambhar and chutney.

Kootu
A thick, creamy, and mildly flavored vegetable dish prepared with dal, ginger, and cumin. Thicker than sambhar, kootus are often served as side dishes in a main meal.

Kulambu
A thick vegetable sauce usually made without dals, kulambu features numerous individual vegetables, and occasionally meats, cooked with tamarind paste and a variety of spices.

Kurma
Exquisitely flavorful vegetable (or meat) sauce made from coconut and almonds ground with many spices to a creamy consistency. A uniquely aromatic and delicious preparation.

Pachadi
Vegetables cooked with a variety of spices in tamarind paste. Similar to kootu, but less creamy in texture, pachadi is a popular accompaniment to a meal.

Payasam
A sweet pudding-like dessert made with milk, cardamom, and saffron. Tapioca or vermicelli are the usual varieties and they are sometimes mixed with fruit cocktail or other fruit.

Podimas
A vegetable dish enhanced with coarsely ground and steamed split peas and spices.

Poori
A bread popular in both South and North India, poori is made with unleavened wheat flour that puffs into airy rounds of bread when deep-fried.

Poriyal
A stir-fried vegetable without sauce that is served as a side dish in a main meal. The vegetables are cooked with seasonings and as a finishing touch combined with dals and coconut.

Rasam
A thin peppery soup made from garlic, onions, and tomatoes, rasam is usually served with rice at mid-course in a meal. It may also be enjoyed at the beginning of a meal. Rasams are believed to relieve the symptoms of colds and sore throats.

Sambhar
Vegetables and dals cooked with sambhar powder to make a hearty sauce of medium or thick consistency. There are a wide variety of sambhars to enjoy with idlis and dosais. Also served in main meals over plain rice.

Uppuma
A popular breakfast or snack item often made from cream of wheat, cream of rice, or cracked wheat seasoned with curry leaves, onions, and spices. Usually served with any sambhar or chutney.

See index for a list of recipes for each dish.

General Cooking Tips

1 Relax and enjoy cooking. Preparing these dishes does not require a precise measurement of the ingredients. If you add a little more or less than the amount specified in the recipe, you are not going to spoil the preparation. Most cooks in India do not use measuring cups or spoons. If you like a certain spice, such as cumin, you may use more than the quantity indicated in the recipe. And if you dislike a particular spice, you may reduce the amount specified in the recipe or omit the ingredient altogether. There are very few absolutely essential spices or seasonings, given the wealth of spices and aromatic ingredients that make up almost every South Indian dish.

2 Indian food is not always hot and spicy. It is the chili peppers and cayenne pepper powder that give the "kick" to a dish. I have indicated only minimal amounts of chili peppers and cayenne pepper powder in my recipes. You may add more or less as you desire.

3 Use plump, ripened, round fresh tomatoes. If you prefer, by adding more fresh tomatoes you can cut down on the prepared tomato sauce you add. In some recipes, however, the tomato sauce enhances the flavor of the vegetable dish and it should not be omitted.

4 Unsweetened shredded coconut, available in Indian grocery stores, can be substituted for freshly ground coconut. Unsweetened coconut powder can be used as a garnish and also as a base for making chutneys and kurmas.

5 Leftovers of most of my dishes can be refrigerated or frozen with no detriment to flavor or nutritional value. Store leftovers in a plastic microwave-safe dish or in a glass container. Just as wine tastes better with age, Indian food often tastes better after a day or two because of the rich blending of spices and seasonings. Most leftovers can be refrigerated for 3 to 5 days or kept frozen for weeks. Just reheat and enjoy.

6 Dals can be cooked in large quantities and kept frozen in one-cup portions for ready use any time. Freeze in a microwave-safe container or any plastic container. Defrost, heat, and use as needed. Cooked dals can be frozen or refrigerated for many weeks with no loss of flavor or nutritional value.

7 Dal should be cooked on the stove or in a pressure cooker to achieve the creamy consistency so desirable for making delicious sambhars and kootus. For poriyals (stir-fry vegetables), however, dals should retain a firmer texture when cooked. Dals cooked in a microwave oven will take an excessive amount of time and will not attain a creamy consistency.

8 The recipes in this book are easy to follow. Once you have assembled all of your ingredients, it usually takes less than thirty minutes to prepare a dish. The more practiced you become in preparing a recipe, the easier it will become.

9 A word about vegetables: Even if you don't like a particular vegetable, you may be surprised at how much its taste is transformed and enhanced when prepared according to the recipes presented in this book. I have found that Brussels sprouts, for example, have won new fans by being prepared in the South Indian-style. Allow this book to expand your taste and that of your family's to include a variety of nutritious vegetables in your daily diet.

10 Here is a hint on using tamarind paste that comes in a bottle: Open the plastic seal and lightly microwave the thick tamarind paste for 1 minute. The paste will be converted to a thick liquid. Now, cover the bottle and store in the kitchen cupboard for any length of time. Tamarind paste, kept at room temperature in this way, is very easy to use.

11 If you are concerned about the amount of time you will need to prepare numerous Indian dishes for a big meal, you can always chop the vegetables ahead of time and keep them refrigerated in plastic wrap, ready for use.

12 You can also make the entire dinner early in the day and leave dishes at room temperature until dinnertime. Advance preparation actually enhances the flavor of the dishes. However, if a dish contains coconut or meat, it is important not to leave the cooked dish at room temperature for an extended period of time. The dish must be refrigerated. Reheat before serving and enjoy.

13 Regular stainless steel heavy-bottomed saucepans, non-stick pots and pans, and healthy ceramic non-stick woks can be used in Indian cooking. Electric rice cookers and woks are useful but not necessary. Electric blenders, however, are necessary.

14 Combining Indian and western dishes makes for a very interesting and pleasing dining experience. Combining grilled chicken or fish with an Indian rice and vegetable dish can be a pleasant change of pace for your family and friends. Be certain to see the section on fusion meals (page 266).

15 Spices are inexpensive, readily available, and have a long shelf life. They do not have to be purchased frequently. When the spices are bought, you just have to take some time to empty them from plastic bags into bottles with lids, label the bottles for familiarity, and store them in the kitchen cabinet.

16 If you don't have a specific spice or other ingredient listed in the recipe, don't be disheartened. It is usually possible to substitute or omit ingredients and still produce a delicious dish, although with a different taste. Here are a few possibilities:

For:	Substitute:
Mustard Seeds and Urad Dal	Cumin Seeds
Urad Dal	Cumin Seeds
Sambhar Powder	Cayenne Pepper Powder and Ground Cumin (in equal parts)
Garam Masala	Curry Powder
Cinnamon sticks	Ground Cinnamon
Rice (White or Brown)	Quinoa or Polenta

Appetizers

Black Bean Cutlets

[Makes 10 cutlets]

 Easy and tasty vegetable cutlet "burgers" can be served as a main course veggie burger or as an appetizer. They are delicious with almost any chutney, but I especially love them with Cilantro Chutney (page 39).

1 (15-ounce) can black beans drained and rinsed (divided)

¼ cup sour cream

2 tablespoons fresh lemon juice

¼ teaspoon ground cumin

¼ teaspoon salt more or less to taste

¼ teaspoon ground black pepper

1 teaspoon garam masala

¼ teaspoon cayenne pepper powder more or less to taste

½ medium onion chopped

2 teaspoons oil

½ cup finely chopped green, red, or yellow bell pepper

½ cup chopped fresh cilantro

½ cup breadcrumbs

1 Put half of the beans in a bowl and reserve. Place the remaining beans in a food processor and add the sour cream, lemon juice, cumin, salt, pepper, garam masala, and cayenne pepper powder and process until smooth.

2 Spoon the bean mixture into the bowl with the reserved beans.

3 Sauté onion in oil on medium heat until translucent. Add bell pepper and cook 1 minute longer while stirring.

4 Add cooked onion and peppers to the bowl with the bean mixture. Add cilantro and breadcrumbs. Stir to blend evenly.

5 Using ¼-cup portions, form the mixture into round patties. Brush or spray the patties with oil and brown on both sides in pan. Serve with chutney.

Chicken Tikka Kebabs

[Makes 8 kebabs]

 Marinated in a vibrant blend of spices, ginger, garlic, and yogurt, these broiled chicken kebabs are especially tender and flavorful. Try them with Cilantro Chutney (page 39).

8 metal or wooden skewers (if using wooden skewers, soak them in water for 30 minutes)

4 boneless skinless chicken thighs or breasts patted dry with paper towels

MARINADE

½ teaspoon cayenne pepper powder

¼ teaspoon ground cardamom

¼ teaspoon dry fenugreek/methi leaves optional

¼ teaspoon curry powder

¼ teaspoon salt more or less to taste

1 tablespoon fresh lemon juice

½ tablespoon grated fresh ginger

½ tablespoon minced garlic cloves

2 tablespoons plain low-fat yogurt

1 Cut the chicken into bite-size cubes.

2 Whisk the marinade ingredients together in a glass bowl. Add the cubed chicken, turning to coat. Cover and marinate for at least 1 hour in the refrigerator, tossing several times.

3 Preheat broiler to 500°F. Line a baking sheet with foil.

4 Thread chicken cubes onto the metal or soaked wooden skewers, leaving about ¼-inch space between each piece to allow for even cooking. Place the skewers of chicken on the baking sheet. Spray chicken lightly with oil.

5 Broil for 15 to 20 minutes, turning halfway through cooking, until chicken is cooked.

Salmon Tikka Kebabs

[Makes 8 kebabs]

 Salmon is a firm fish that combines beautifully with Indian spices. These salmon cubes are marinated in spiced yogurt and broiled for an enticing appetizer. Serve with Seasoned Apple Relish (page 42).

8 metal or wooden skewers (if using wooden skewers, soak them in water for 30 minutes)

1 pound boneless skinless wild salmon filet cut into bite-size cubes

MARINADE

½ teaspoon cayenne pepper powder more or less to taste

½ teaspoon Black Pepper and Cumin Powder (page 4)

¼ teaspoon curry powder

¼ teaspoon salt more or less to taste

1 tablespoon fresh lemon juice

½ tablespoon grated fresh ginger

½ tablespoon minced garlic cloves

2 tablespoons plain low-fat yogurt

1 Whisk the marinade ingredients in a glass bowl. Add the cubed salmon and toss to coat. Cover and refrigerate for 1 hour, stirring several times.

2 Preheat broiler to 500°F. Line a baking sheet with foil.

3 Thread marinated salmon cubes onto the metal or soaked wooden skewers, leaving about ¼-inch space between pieces to allow for even cooking. Place the skewers of salmon on the baking sheet. Spray the salmon lightly with oil.

4 Broil for 12 to 15 minutes, turning halfway through cooking.

Potato Cutlets

[Makes 14 cutlets]

 Delicious seasoned mashed potatoes are used to prepare these crispy golden brown cutlets.

2 medium Idaho potatoes with skins cut in quarters

½ teaspoon ground turmeric divided

1 teaspoon salt divided

2 tablespoons oil

¼ teaspoon asafoetida powder

2 to 4 curry leaves optional

½ teaspoon black mustard seeds

½ teaspoon urad dal

1 cup chopped onions

½ cup chopped tomatoes

1 fresh green chili pepper chopped

1 tablespoon minced fresh ginger

½ teaspoon cayenne pepper powder

¼ cup minced fresh cilantro leaves

1 Use the ingredients to prepare Potato Masala as instructed on page 201 and then let the mixture cool.

2 Preheat oven to 400°F.

3 Using 1 tablespoon of potato mixture for each cutlet, form into balls and flatten into round cutlets. Spray cutlets with cooking spray or brush with oil.

4 Place the cutlets on a baking sheet. Bake on each side for 3 to 5 minutes. (If desired, cook in a skillet: place potato cutlets in a lightly-oiled, heated skillet and brown the cutlets on both sides until golden brown.)

Roasted Vegetable Kebabs

[Makes 8 kebabs]

 Roasting brings out the slightly sweet flavors of vegetables. Combined with aromatic spices, they make a tasty, nutritious appetizer or side dish. Serve with Peanut and Coconut Chutney (page 43).

8 metal or wooden skewers (if using wooden skewers, soak them in water for 30 minutes)

1 tablespoon oil

½ teaspoon ground cumin

1 teaspoon curry powder

½ teaspoon smoked paprika or **⅛ teaspoon cayenne pepper powder** more or less to taste

¼ teaspoon salt more or less to taste

2½ cups vegetables cut into pieces, such as:

½ medium zucchini cut in half lengthwise, then in half circles

½ medium yellow squash cut in half lengthwise, then in half circles

1 cup red, green, and/or yellow bell pepper cubes

½ cup baby portabella mushrooms cut in half

1 Preheat oven to 425°F.

2 In a plastic resealable bag combine oil, cumin, curry powder, smoked paprika (or cayenne), and salt. Add vegetables, seal, and turn bag several times until spices and oil are evenly distributed.

3 Thread vegetables onto skewers alternating varieties.

4 Place kebabs in a single layer on a heavy-duty rimmed baking sheet. (Dark baking sheets work best to brown vegetables; do not use a light-colored pan or aluminum foil as they prevent vegetables from browning quickly.)

5 Place in oven and roast about 7 minutes. Check to see if they are starting to brown. If not, return to the oven for 3 to 5 more minutes.

6 Turn and bake about 7 minutes longer or until vegetables are cooked as you like them. The time will vary based on your individual oven and the vegetables used.

Savory Tuna Masala

[Serves 4]

 Here's a delicious twist on tuna salad that can be served as an appetizer with rice crackers or spread on toasted bread for a sandwich. Sautéing the onions and tomatoes with the aromatics brings out the flavors of the spices, and chopped nuts add crunch. Tuna Masala also makes a great main dish served with rice and vegetables, or a delicious filling for Stuffed Baby Portabella Mushrooms (page 33).

2 tablespoons oil

3 (½-inch-long) slivers cinnamon stick

½ teaspoon fennel seeds

½ teaspoon cumin seeds

1 cup chopped onions

½ cup finely chopped tomatoes

1 tablespoon minced garlic cloves

½ teaspoon ground turmeric

2 teaspoons curry powder

½ teaspoon ground cumin

¼ teaspoon salt more or less to taste

3 tablespoons tomato sauce

1 (9-ounce) can light tuna, packed in water
  drained

1 (5-ounce) can light tuna, packed in oil
  drained

2 tablespoons chopped walnuts or peanuts
  optional

2 tablespoons minced fresh cilantro

1 Heat oil in a skillet over medium-high heat. When the oil is hot but not smoking, add cinnamon stick, fennel seeds, and cumin seeds; stir about a minute until cumin seeds change color from light brown to semi-dark brown.

2 Add onions, tomatoes, and garlic. Cook for 1 minute. Add turmeric, curry powder, ground cumin, and salt. Cook for 1 minute while stirring. Stir in tomato sauce.

3 Add tuna, mix thoroughly and continue to cook 5 minutes over medium-low heat.

4 Remove from heat and stir in walnuts and cilantro.

Spinach Yogurt Dip

[Makes 1½ cups]

 This zesty, creamy dip tastes indulgent but is actually packed with healthful ingredients—seasoned fresh baby spinach, garlic, ginger, coconut, and yogurt. You can serve it as a dip with vegetables, rice crackers, or pita triangles and it also works well as a side dish.

1 teaspoon oil

1 teaspoon black mustard seeds

½ teaspoon cumin seeds or **urad dal**

½ cup chopped onions

¼ **of a fresh green chili** minced (more or less to taste)

1 tablespoon minced garlic cloves

1 tablespoon grated fresh ginger

4 cups baby spinach chopped

1 teaspoon ground cumin

¼ teaspoon salt more or less to taste

1 tablespoon grated fresh coconut or unsweetened shredded coconut

¾ cup plain low-fat yogurt

1 Heat oil in a skillet over medium-high heat. When the oil is hot but not smoking, add mustard seeds and cumin seeds or urad dal and stir until mustard seeds start to pop and cumin seeds change color from light brown to semi-dark brown, about 30 seconds.

2 Add onions, green chili, garlic, and ginger and cook for 1 to 2 minutes while stirring.

3 Add spinach, ground cumin, and salt. Mix well and cook until spinach is slightly wilted. Add coconut and mix well. *At this point you can serve it as a side vegetable to any meal!*

4 Place the spinach in a bowl and allow to cool. Stir the yogurt into the cooled spinach. Serve as a dip or side dish (**Seasoned Fresh Spinach in Yogurt**) at room temperature or store in the refrigerator and serve cold.

Stuffed Baby Portabella Mushrooms

[Makes 12]

 "Baby bella" or baby portabella mushrooms have a meaty, firm flesh and appealing woodsy flavor. Mushroom lovers will delight in these mushrooms filled with spinach or tuna. They are perfect for entertaining because they can be made ahead and refrigerated until you are ready to bake them.

12 baby portabella mushrooms or **regular white mushrooms**

¼ cup Spinach Poriyal with Lentils and Coconut (page 211) or **Savory Tuna Masala** (page 29)

1 tablespoon finely minced roasted red bell pepper (from a jar)

1 Preheat oven to 350°F.

2 Wipe mushrooms with a damp paper towel. Carefully remove stems. Use the small end of a melonball scoop to fill mushroom cups with spinach or tuna mixture. Top with a few pieces of red pepper.

3 Place stuffed mushrooms on a baking sheets and spray them with cooking spray. Bake, uncovered, for 12 to 15 minutes.

Chutneys & Sauces

Eggplant Chutney

[Makes 2 cups]

 This is a simpler version of traditional Eggplant Chutney.

2 tablespoons oil

1 whole dried red chili pepper more, if desired

2 cups unpeeled chopped eggplant

½ cup coarsely chopped onions

½ cup coarsely chopped tomatoes

2 garlic cloves peeled and cut in half

½ teaspoon ground turmeric

2 thin slices fresh ginger

½ cup tomato sauce

½ teaspoon salt more, if desired

½ cup warm water

½ teaspoon tamarind paste diluted with ½ teaspoon water; or ½ teaspoon fresh lemon juice

1 Place oil in a warmed skillet. When oil is hot, add red chili pepper, eggplant, onions, tomatoes, and garlic. Stir-fry for about 2 minutes.

2 Add turmeric, ginger, and tomato sauce. Stir well. Add salt. Cover and cook over medium heat until eggplant becomes soft, about 5 to 7 minutes.

3 Transfer mixture from skillet to a blender or food processor and grind. Add warm water and grind to a thick paste.

4 Transfer eggplant mixture to a serving bowl and stir in tamarind paste or lemon juice. Mix well. Serve or refrigerate until ready to serve.

Cilantro Chutney I

[Makes 1 cup]

 You probably know this vibrant green chutney as a staple of Indian cuisine. My versions are creamy with the addition of yogurt and buttermilk. Easy to prepare, cilantro chutney is packed with flavor. It can be served as an accompaniment to many appetizers; or with breakfast items such as idlis, dosais, and uppumas; or as a spread on a sandwich.

¼ cup chopped onions

1 tablespoon grated fresh ginger

2 cups coarsely chopped fresh cilantro leaves and stems

1 fresh green chili pepper chopped (more or less to taste)

6 whole almonds

¼ cup unsweetened shredded coconut

½ cup plain yogurt

½ cup buttermilk or water

¼ teaspoon salt more or less to taste

1 teaspoon fresh lemon juice

Place onions, ginger, cilantro, chili, almonds, coconut, yogurt, and buttermilk or water in a blender or food processor. Grind and process until a smooth, thick consistency. Add salt and lemon juice. Process to blend well. Transfer to a bowl. Refrigerate until ready to serve (can keep for 2 to 3 days).

Cilantro Chutney II

¼ cup chopped onions

2 cups chopped fresh cilantro leaves and stems

1 or 2 fresh green chili peppers

¼ teaspoon cumin seeds

2 tablespoons unsweetened shredded coconut

½ teaspoon salt

¼ teaspoon tamarind paste

½ cup plain yogurt

½ cup buttermilk or water

Combine all the ingredients in a blender and grind to a smooth, thick consistency. Store in refrigerator until ready to serve (can keep for 2 to 3 days).

To enhance the flavor, after the cilantro chutney is prepared, and just before serving: Heat 1 tablespoon oil in a small saucepan. When oil is hot, but not smoking add 1 dried whole red pepper, ½ teaspoon black mustard seeds, and ½ teaspoon urad dal. Sauté until seeds pop and urad dal turns golden, about 30 seconds. Add the sautéed seasonings to the chutney.

Kosamalli (Seasoned Eggplant Sauce)

[Serves 4]

 This seasoned eggplant sauce is a specialty of the Chettinad region of South India. Eggplant is cooked to perfection with onions and tomatoes in tamarind sauce. Kosamalli is usually served with adais (page 61), idlis (page 73), dosais (page 65), or idiyappam (page 71).

3 cups chopped eggplant with skin

1 cup chopped onions

¼ cup chopped tomatoes

1 fresh green chili pepper chopped (more, if desired)

2 tablespoons oil

4 to 6 curry leaves

¼ teaspoon asafoetida powder

1 teaspoon black mustard seeds

1 teaspoon urad dal

¼ teaspoon ground turmeric

½ teaspoon cayenne pepper powder

½ teaspoon ground cumin

1 teaspoon salt

¼ teaspoon tamarind paste

½ cup tomato sauce

¼ cup chopped fresh cilantro leaves

1 Put the chopped eggplant in a saucepan with 3 cups of water. Cook, uncovered, for a few minutes until eggplant becomes soft. Mash undrained eggplant and set aside. (You could peel eggplant if you prefer not to use the skin.)

2 Combine onions, tomatoes, and green chili pepper in a small bowl and set aside.

3 Heat oil in a saucepan over medium heat. When oil is hot, but not smoking, add curry leaves, asafoetida powder, mustard seeds, and urad dal. Fry until mustard seeds pop and urad dal turns golden brown, about 30 seconds.

4 Immediately add onion mixture and cook until onions are tender.

5 Add the turmeric and mix well. Add the mashed eggplant and stir to combine. Add cayenne pepper powder, cumin, salt, tamarind paste, and tomato sauce and stir to combine.

6 Add 2 cups of water and stir. When the mixture begins to boil, add the cilantro leaves and let sauce simmer over medium heat for 5 to 7 minutes.

Seasoned Apple Relish

[Makes 1 cup / Serves 4]

 There are so many ways to enjoy this apple relish with a kick. You can spread it on toast or crackers for a savory-sweet snack, or it works well with grilled or baked fish or chicken as a side relish!

2 tablespoons oil

1 teaspoon black mustard seeds

1 Granny Smith apple unpeeled and shredded

½ teaspoon ground turmeric

¼ teaspoon ground cumin

¼ teaspoon cayenne pepper powder more or less to taste

¼ teaspoon salt more or less to taste

1 Heat oil in a skillet over medium-high heat. When the oil is hot but not smoking, add mustard seeds and cook and stir until seeds start to pop.

2 Add apple, turmeric, cumin, cayenne pepper powder, and salt. Cover and cook 2 to 3 minutes.

3 Scrape into a dish and serve warm or cold.

Variation
To make **Creamy Apple Chutney Dip** add plain, low-fat yogurt. Use an equal measure of yogurt to relish. It makes a great dip with vegetables.

Peanut and Coconut Chutney

[Makes 1½ cups]

 Unlike peanut butter, this savory peanut chutney gets a little heat from red chili pepper! Try it spread on sandwiches or served as a dip for fresh vegetables.

1 cup dry-roasted unsalted peanuts

¼ **cup grated fresh coconut** or **unsweetened dried coconut**

3 **garlic cloves** peeled and cut in half

1 **whole dried red chili pepper** more or less to taste

¼ **teaspoon salt** more or less to taste

¾ **to 1 cup warm water**

1 Place peanuts, coconut, garlic cloves, chili pepper, salt, and ¾ cup warm water in a blender or food processor; blend or process until smooth.

2 If the chutney seems too thick, add additional water, 1 tablespoon at a time. Scrape into a dish and serve.

Potato Onion Kose

[Serves 6]

 This hearty tomato-based sauce with potatoes is a Chettinad speciality! An excellent accompaniment to any breads, adais (page 61), idlis (page 73), or dosais (page 65).

2 tablespoons oil

2 to 4 (½-inch-long) slivers cinnamon stick

1 bay leaf

½ teaspoon black mustard seeds

½ teaspoon urad dal

½ cup chopped onions

½ cup chopped tomatoes

1 cup ½-inch pieces peeled potatoes

¼ teaspoon ground turmeric

½ teaspoon cayenne pepper powder

1 teaspoon ground cumin

½ cup tomato sauce

½ teaspoon salt

¼ cup chopped fresh cilantro leaves

1 Heat oil in a medium saucepan over medium heat. When oil is hot, but not smoking, add cinnamon sticks, bay leaf, mustard seeds, and urad dal. Cover and cook until mustard seeds pop and urad dal is golden brown, about 30 seconds.

2 Immediately add onion, tomato, potatoes and turmeric to saucepan and stir well. Cook, uncovered, over medium-low heat for 1 to 2 minutes.

3 Add cayenne, cumin, tomato sauce, and salt. Stir well. Add 2 cups of water and stir well. When the ingredients start to boil, add cilantro. Cook, covered, over medium-low heat until potatoes are tender, 8 to 10 minutes, stirring frequently.

Tomato and Onion Chutney

[Makes 1 cup]

 This bright, zesty chutney is an excellent staple to keep on hand. It adds instant flavor as a spread in sandwiches, or it can be served alongside grilled or baked meat dishes.

2 tablespoons oil

1 whole dried red chili pepper more or less to taste

½ teaspoon black mustard seeds

½ teaspoon urad dal

½ cup chopped onions

½ cup chopped tomatoes

¼ teaspoon ground turmeric

¼ teaspoon cayenne pepper powder more or less to taste

¼ teaspoon ground cumin

¼ teaspoon salt more or less to taste

½ cup tomato sauce

1 tablespoon minced fresh cilantro

1 Heat oil in a skillet over medium-high heat. When the oil is hot but not smoking, add chili pepper, mustard seeds, and urad dal and stir a minute or two until mustard seeds start to pop.

2 Add onion and tomatoes to skillet; cook and stir until onions are translucent.

3 Add turmeric, cayenne, cumin, and salt. Stir and cook for a few minutes until mixture is well-blended.

4 Stir in tomato sauce and 2 tablespoons water. Cook for a minute or two. Stir in cilantro. This chutney can be stored in the refrigerator for up to 2 days.

Soups

Carrot and Lentil Soup with Kale

[Serves 4 to 6]

 This hearty, fiber-rich vegan soup is a meal unto itself. Lentil soup gets a makeover with aromatic ginger, spices, and kale.

½ **medium onion** chopped

½ **tablespoon oil**

½ **pound (2 to 3 medium) carrots** peeled and chopped

1 **garlic clove** finely chopped

½ **tablespoon grated fresh ginger**

½ **fresh green chili pepper** chopped (more or less to taste / for less "heat" use green bell pepper)

½ **cup masoor dal (red lentils)**

2½ **cups reduced-sodium vegetable broth**

1 **cup low-sodium spicy vegetable juice** or 1 **cup water with about ¼ teaspoon cayenne pepper powder added**

½ **teaspoon ground turmeric**

½ **teaspoon ground cumin**

1 **cup chopped kale leaves** stems discarded

1 **tablespoon minced fresh cilantro**

1 In a 4-quart stockpot over medium heat, sauté the onion in the oil until softened.

2 Add carrots, garlic, ginger, chili pepper, and masoor dal, and sauté for a few minutes.

3 Add broth, vegetable juice (or water and cayenne), turmeric, and cumin. Bring to a boil, then reduce to a simmer, cover, and cook for 15 to 20 minutes or until carrots are as soft as you like them.

4 Add kale and cook 3 more minutes.

5 If soup is too thick, add up to 2 cups of hot water till desired thickness. Simmer on low-medium heat for 3 minutes. Serve garnished with cilantro.

Cauliflower and Lentil Soup

[Serves 4 to 6]

 Red lentils add protein and fiber to this aromatic dal-based soup, which features cauliflower and tomatoes. The flavors of cinnamon and cardamom give this soup a lovely depth. It is a perfect lunch on a chilly day!

¼ **cup masoor dal (red lentils)** or **moong dal (split yellow mung beans)**

½ **teaspoon ground turmeric** divided

2 **tablespoons oil**

3 **(½-inch-long) slivers cinnamon stick**

1 **bay leaf**

½ **medium onion** sliced lengthwise

1 **cup chopped tomatoes**

½ **fresh green chili pepper** minced (more or less to taste)

½ **cup tomato sauce**

4 **cups hot water**

¼ **teaspoon ground cardamom** optional

2 **teaspoons ground cumin**

½ **teaspoon salt** more or less to taste

2 **cups (1-inch pieces) cauliflower florets**

2 **tablespoons minced fresh cilantro**

1 Bring 2 cups of water to a boil in a deep saucepan. Add lentils and ¼ teaspoon turmeric. Reduce heat to medium and cook, uncovered, for about 30 minutes, until lentils are soft and creamy. Do not drain. Reserve.

2 Heat oil in a deep saucepan over medium heat. When the oil is hot but not smoking, add cinnamon stick and bay leaf and stir a few seconds.

3 Add onion slices, tomatoes, green chili pepper, and remaining ¼ teaspoon turmeric. Cook and stir, uncovered, until onions and tomatoes are tender.

4 Add tomato sauce and reserved lentils with water. Stir in 4 cups of hot water. Add cardamom, cumin, and salt and stir well. Cook, uncovered, over medium heat until mixture begins to boil.

5 Reduce heat. Add cauliflower and cook, uncovered, about 2 minutes or until cauliflower is just tender. Do not overcook cauliflower.

6 Add cilantro, simmer a few minutes. Remove from heat. Serve immediately or cover and set aside off heat until ready to serve. Briefly reheat before serving.

VARIATION
You can use about **1 cup sliced beets** in place of the cauliflower and follow the above recipe to make **Beet & Lentil Soup**.

Peppery Lemon Soup

[Serves 4]

 Ginger and garlic pair with lemon and chilies in a light lentil-based soup.
It is a perfect way to warm up and ward away colds!

¼ cup masoor dal (red lentils)

½ teaspoon ground turmeric divided

1 cup chopped tomatoes

½ tablespoon grated fresh ginger

½ fresh green chili pepper chopped (more or less to taste)

1 garlic clove crushed

½ teaspoon salt more or less to taste

¼ teaspoon Black Pepper and Cumin Powder (page 4)

2 teaspoons fresh lemon juice

2 tablespoons chopped fresh cilantro

1 Bring 2 cups of water to a boil in a 2-quart saucepan. Add masoor dal and ¼ teaspoon turmeric. Reduce heat to medium and cook, uncovered, for about 20 minutes, until dal become soft and fall apart. If water evaporates during the cooking process, add another cup of water.

2 Add the remaining ¼ teaspoon ground turmeric, tomatoes, ginger, chili pepper, and garlic and cook over medium-low heat for 2 to 3 minutes.

3 Add 2 cups of water, the salt, and Black Pepper and Cumin Powder. Bring to a boil and then reduce heat and simmer for 3 to 5 minutes.

4 Remove from heat; add lemon juice and cilantro. Stir and serve.

VARIATION
To make **Peppery Lemon Shrimp Soup**, add **½ pound raw shrimp**, shelled and cleaned and cut in half, in Step 3 once you have reduced heat, and let simmer for 5 to 7 minutes.

Sweet Potato Quinoa Soup

[Serves 6]

 Quinoa is not actually a grain, but rather the seeds of a green leafy plant. It is gluten-free and rich in protein. Quinoa, sweet potatoes, corn, and two kinds of beans come together beautifully in this hearty soup.

½ cup **quinoa**

1 medium **onion** chopped

2 teaspoons **oil**

5 cups **reduced-sodium vegetable or chicken broth**

2 teaspoons **ground cumin**

½ teaspoon **ground turmeric**

¼ teaspoon **cayenne pepper powder** more or less to taste

1 cup **fresh cut green beans**

¼ cup **frozen corn**

2 cups **peeled and cubed sweet potatoes**

1 (15-ounce) can **reduced-sodium white beans (cannellini, navy, or chickpeas)** drained and rinsed

¼ cup **chopped fresh cilantro**

1 Rinse quinoa in several changes of water and drain in a fine-mesh strainer. Reserve.

2 In a 3-quart saucepan over medium heat, sauté onion in oil about 3 minutes or until onion is translucent. Add reserved quinoa and stir for a few minutes.

3 Add broth, cumin, turmeric, and cayenne. Bring to a boil, then reduce heat, cover, and simmer for 10 minutes.

4 Add green beans, corn, and sweet potatoes. Bring back to a boil, then reduce heat, cover, and simmer for 5 to 10 minutes, until sweet potatoes are tender.

5 Add white beans and cilantro; heat for 2 minutes and serve.

Breakfast

Adais

[Makes 15 crepes / Serves 4 to 6]

 Adais are multigrain, gluten-free lentil crepes packed with nutrition. Adai batter does not require fermentation. These crepes are easy to prepare and are typically served with any type of chutney or Kosamalli (page 41). Adais also make a wonderful sandwich wrap—spread with fillings and chutney, roll up, and enjoy.

½ cup yellow split peas

¼ cup masoor dal (red lentils)

½ cup moong dal (split yellow mung beans)

½ cup extra-long-grain rice

2 whole dried red chili peppers more or less to taste

1 teaspoon cumin seeds

1 teaspoon fennel seeds

½ teaspoon ground turmeric

½ teaspoon salt more or less to taste

½ cup minced onion

1 tablespoon minced fresh ginger

¼ cup chopped fresh cilantro

1 Soak the yellow split peas, masoor dal, moong dal, rice, red chili peppers, cumin seeds, and fennel seeds in 3 cups of water for 2 hours. Drain and discard water.

2 Place soaked mixture in a blender with 1½ cups of fresh water. Add turmeric, salt, onion, and ginger. Grind to a coarse, thick consistency adding additional water, a tablespoon at a time, if needed. (The batter should be quite thick; you can add more water when making crepes if needed.)

3 Add cilantro and blend a few seconds. The mixture is ready for making the crepes.

4 Heat a skillet over medium heat. Brush with ¼ teaspoon oil or spray with cooking spray. Using ¼ cup of batter for each crepe, spread the batter in the skillet in a circular pattern with the back of a spoon, as thinly as possible. Cook until the crepe becomes crunchy and golden. Loosen the edges with a spatula. Turn over and cook until golden brown, about 1 minute longer. Adjust heat as necessary for even browning. Roll or fold and serve hot.

Cream of Wheat Uppuma

[Serves 4]

 This is a savory, flavorful version of Cream of Wheat cooked with onions and spices. You can serve this uppuma with a sambhar or a chutney. This recipe is often enjoyed for breakfast or at afternoon tea.

2 tablespoons oil

1 whole dried red chili pepper

1 teaspoon black mustard seeds

1 teaspoon urad dal

¼ cup finely chopped onions

¼ cup finely chopped tomatoes

1 cup uncooked quick or regular cream of wheat*

½ teaspoon salt

1 fresh green chili pepper finely chopped

2 teaspoons minced fresh ginger

2 cups warm water

¼ cup minced fresh cilantro leaves

1 teaspoon unsalted butter

2 tablespoons roasted cashew halves
optional

*Cream of wheat can be replaced with **cracked wheat** (crushed or cut raw wheat kernels, often available with specialty flours) or **quinoa**.

1 Place oil in a skillet over medium heat. When oil is hot, but not smoking, add red chili pepper, mustard seeds, and urad dal and cook for a few seconds until urad dal turns golden.

2 Add onions and tomatoes and cook for 1 minute. Add cream of wheat and stir for 1 minute. Add salt, chili pepper, and ginger. Stir for 1 minute.

3 Gradually add 2 cups of warm water to cream of wheat while stirring. Cover and cook over low heat, stirring frequently, for about 2 minutes.

4 Add cilantro and butter. Stir well. Add cashews, if desired, and mix well.

VARIATION

To make **Vegetable Uppuma**, follow the same recipe but after adding water to cream of wheat, add **¼ cup shredded carrots** and **¼ cup frozen (thawed) green peas** and stir. Cover and cook over low heat stirring frequently.

There are 4 steps to making dosais:
1. Soaking the ingredients for about 3 hours
2. Grinding for less than 15 minutes
3. Fermenting for 6 to 8 hours (overnight)
4. Cooking dosais (only 3 minutes at most)

Fermenting Note:
Sometimes, because of cold weather, the dosai batter will not ferment. You may place the bowl in a warmed oven to facilitate: just preheat oven to 350 degrees for 10 minutes and then turn off the oven; wait 10 to 15 minutes, then place the bowl with batter, still covered, in the oven.

Sometimes, depending upon the temperature and humidity, you might have the opposite problem and the batter might ferment in a shorter time and may overflow from the mixing bowl. This will still result in good dosais. Discard the overflow (it cleans up easily) and work with the batter in the bowl.

Plain Dosais

[Makes 16 dosais]

 Thin unsweetened pancakes made of rice and urad dal, dosais are a delicious breakfast item that are also served for afternoon tea or for a light evening meal. Unique to South India, dosais can be made plain or as onion dosais or masala dosais (page 67). Serve any variety hot with a chutney or sambhar.

The batter for dosais has to ferment for 6 to 8 hours, so requires planning ahead. Grind the batter a day before you intend to prepare them in order for fermentation to take place. You may make a few dosais at a time. Save the remaining batter in the refrigerator for making dosais at a later time. The batter can be kept for several days in the refrigerator, but do not freeze.

2 cups uncooked extra-long-grain rice

½ cup urad dal

1 teaspoon fenugreek seeds (optional)

½ cup cooked plain rice

1 teaspoon salt

1½ cups warm water

1 Place uncooked rice, urad dal, and fenugreek seeds in warm water to cover. Stir the mixture with your fingers, rubbing it gently to loosen the starches from the grains. Drain and repeat 2 or 3 times until water runs clear. Add enough warm water to cover generously and soak at room temperature for about 3 hours.

2 Drain water and place rice mixture in an electric blender. Add a little warm water to facilitate the grinding process. Grind on high power for several minutes, adding cooked rice a little at a time as it is being ground until you have a fine paste (cooked rice is added to improve the texture of the batter).

3 Pour the creamy fine batter into a deep mixing bowl (be certain that the bowl you are using will allow the batter to double its quantity). Add the salt and mix well with your hand. (It is essential to use your hand for mixing and not a spoon, because the warmth of the hand initiates the fermentation process.)

4 Cover the bowl with a plate and put it in a warm place in the kitchen overnight. (You can also turn just the oven light on and leave the ground batter inside the oven overnight.) Do not use direct heat. The rice batter will begin to ferment and will double in quantity.

5 The next morning the fermented batter will be frothy. Stir the batter with a large spoon for a few minutes and set aside. Now you are ready to make dosais.

To Cook Plain Dosais:

6 Place about ½ cup of batter into the center of a hot 10-inch nonstick skillet. Spread the batter with a spoon by moving it in concentric circles, starting at the inside of the circle and working towards the outside, spreading the batter thinly and evenly.

7 Cover and cook over medium heat for 1 to 2 minutes. To make plain, soft dosai cook only on one side. If added crispiness is desired, when tiny bubbles appear on the dosai in the skillet place about ½ to 1 teaspoon canola oil in the pan around the dosai. Lift the dosai with a spatula and turn over in skillet. After both sides are cooked evenly, transfer the dosai to a serving plate. Repeat with remaining batter.

Dosais are often served folded in a semicircular shape.

The dosai batter can also be used to make uthappams (page 69).

Masala Dosais

[Makes 16 dosais]

 These dosais are stuffed with cilantro chutney and potato masala.

1 batch Plain Dosais batter (page 65)
1 batch Cilantro Chutney (page 39)
1 batch Potato Masala (page 201)
¼ to ½ teaspoon butter or margarine melted

1 Make the batter for Plain Dosais. (Note: this needs to be done the day before.)

2 Heat a 10-inch nonstick skillet. Spread a ½ cup batter in the skillet as instructed in Step 6 of Plain Dosais recipe.

3 With a spoon, spread some cilantro chutney evenly over top of the dosai. Place 1 to 2 tablespoons of potato masala over the cilantro chutney on one half of the dosai only. Fold the dosai up over the potato mixture and pat down with spatula. The dosai should now have a semicircular shape.

4 Lightly brush the dosai with melted butter and brown evenly one side at a time until desired crispness is reached.

5 Remove dosai to serving platter and repeat the same procedure with the rest of the batter.

Note: Be certain to wipe all butter from skillet with a paper towel before you start making the next dosai, otherwise the batter will not spread evenly in the skillet.

Uthappams

[Makes 12 uthappams]

 Uthappams are a thicker variety of dosai, typically garnished with onions, chilies, and cilantro. They make a flavorful breakfast treat.

1 batch Plain Dosais batter (page 65)
6 to 12 teaspoons canola oil
Finely chopped onion
Finely chopped fresh green chili peppers
Finely chopped fresh cilantro

1 Make the batter for Plain Dosais. (Note: this needs to be done the day before.)

1 Heat a nonstick skillet or iron skillet over medium heat. If you are using an iron skillet, spray with nonstick cooking spray.

2 Pour ½ cup of the dosai batter in the middle of the hot skillet and spread it like a small thick pancake about 6 inches in diameter.

3 When tiny bubbles appear on the uthappam in the skillet place ½ to 1 teaspoon oil in the pan around the uthappam. Sprinkle chopped onion, chili peppers, and cilantro over the uthappam as it cooks. After about 1 minute, turn the uthappam to the other side and cook until the uthappam becomes golden brown.

Idiyappam

[Serves 4 to 6]

 These seasoned rice noodles are a delicate dish made with thin rice sticks. Idiyappam served with Carrot Sambhar (page 123) or Kosamalli (page 41) is a delicious way to start the day!

1 pound thin rice sticks*

2 teaspoons salt

4 tablespoons plus 1 teaspoon canola oil

5 or 6 curry leaves

3 teaspoons black mustard seeds

3 teaspoons urad dal

2 onions chopped

2 fresh green chili peppers chopped

¼ cup low-fat buttermilk

¼ cup fresh cilantro leaves chopped

*Dynasty brand Maifun "Rice Sticks" (6.75 oz.) are available in most grocery stores and Thai markets.

1 Remove rice sticks from package and break into small pieces.

2 Bring 6 to 8 cups of water to a boil in a large saucepan. When water is boiling vigorously, add salt, 1 teaspoon oil, and rice sticks. Boil, uncovered, for about 5 minutes. Do not overcook. (Oil is added to the boiling water to prevent rice sticks from sticking together.) When rice sticks are tender, drain thoroughly in a colander. Set aside.

3 Place remaining 4 tablespoons canola oil in a large skillet and heat over medium heat. When oil is hot, but not smoking, add curry leaves, mustard seeds, and urad dal. Cover and cook until mustard seeds pop and urad dal is golden brown, about 30 seconds.

4 Add onions and chili peppers to skillet. Stir-fry for a few minutes. Add drained rice sticks and reduce heat to low while mixing well.

5 Add buttermilk to moisten rice sticks slightly. Stir delicately and add more salt, if desired. Stir in cilantro and serve.

Traditional Idlis

[Makes 20]

 Idlis are light, steamed rice cakes. To make them you will need an idli cooker, which is available in Indian grocery stores. Plan to soak, grind, and ferment the batter a day in advance. The special rice for making them, called "idli rice," is also available in Indian grocery stores.

2 cups idli rice
½ cup urad dal
1 teaspoon salt

Equipment: idli cooker

1 Put the rice and urad dal in two separate bowls. Rinse the rice and urad dal separately, rubbing them with your fingers gently to loosen the starches from the grains. Drain and repeat 2 to 3 times until water runs clear. After rinsing, add enough warm water to generously cover each and let soak separately for 3 hours.

2 Drain the soaked rice and put the rice in a blender with enough water to facilitate grinding (about 1½ cups). Grind to a coarse cornmeal-like texture. Transfer ground rice to a deep bowl.

3 Drain water from soaked urad dal and place urad dal in the blender. Add just enough water (about 1½ cups) to facilitate grinding. Grind to a fine smooth paste. Transfer ground dal to the deep bowl with the rice.

4 Add salt to the rice/dal mixture. With your hand, mix the batters and the salt thoroughly. (It is important to use your hand and not a spoon, because the warmth from your hand will start the fermentation process of the batter.)

5 Cover the bowl and set aside in a warm place overnight but do not use direct heat.

6 The following morning, or about 6 hours later depending upon the outside temperature and humidity, you will notice that the batter has risen in the bowl and has a foamy appearance. This is fermentation. It is important not to stir the batter after fermentation. The batter is now ready for you to make idlis with an idli cooker.

7 The idli cooker is a special type of vessel that is used to make idlis. It has a bottom pan to hold water and a plate insert with 5 to 7 mold sections, similar in appearance to an egg poacher. A wet cloth is draped over the idli plate and the batter is poured into each mold over the steamed cloth. The steamed cloth is necessary to stop the batter from flowing into the water in the bottom vessel. The vessel has a tight cover to steam cook the idlis. Follow the directions given with the idli cooker and steam cook for 8 to 10 minutes.

Fermenting Note:
Sometimes in cold weather the batter may not readily ferment. To encourage the fermentation process, place the bowl in a warmed oven using the following directions: first heat oven to 350 degrees for 10 minutes and then turn it off; after 10 to 15 minutes, the bowl with batter can be placed, still covered, in the oven. You may also use the warmth of the oven light to promote fermentation without turning on the oven: place the bowl with batter inside the oven with oven light on for 4 to 6 hours.

Pooris

[Makes about 12 / Serves 4]

 Pooris, unleavened Indian wheat breads, are similar to chapatti or roti, except that they are deep-fried. The layers of the bread puff up as they fry and they are always a welcome treat at my table. Pooris can be enjoyed for breakfast, or as a snack or light meal. Serve with potato masala as a side dish.

1 cup graham wheat flour*
1 teaspoon oil
½ teaspoon salt
¾ cup warm water
Oil for frying

*Pooris can also be made with King Arthur brand 100% wholewheat flour using approximately 1 cup warm water.

1 Place the flour, oil, and salt in a large bowl and mix well with your hand. Add warm water to flour mixture a little at a time and work ingredients with your hands until they form a firm dough without sticking to your fingers.

2 Knead the dough well with lightly oiled hands. Pound dough vigorously into bowl several times. (A food processor may also be used to form the dough.)

3 Roll the dough into a long, cord-like shape using the palms of both hands. Break off small pieces of dough and form into small, smooth balls, approximately the size of a walnut. If large pooris are desired, the dough should be formed into larger equal-size balls.

4 Dab a very small amount of oil on a flat board or work surface. Place a ball of dough on oiled surface and flatten evenly into a disc approximately 3 inches in diameter.

5 Heat about 2 inches of oil in a small wok. When oil is hot enough (the pooris will puff up only if the oil is hot enough but not smoking), drop one poori into the oil (it is best to fry them one at a time). The poori will sizzle and rise to the surface. Using a slotted spoon, turn the poori over and fry for an additional 10 to 15 seconds until light golden brown.

6 Lift the poori out of the pan with a slotted spoon, drain off the excess oil on paper towels. Repeat with remaning discs. Serve hot.

Rice & Quinoa

Notes about Rice and Quinoa

RICE

Rice is a staple food of South India. The types of rice commonly used in our recipes for rice dishes are basmati, jasmine, and extra-long-grain (see page 6 for descriptions of these varieties).

BASIC COOKING INSTRUCTIONS FOR RICE
In a Rice Cooker:
To cook any type of rice, I highly recommend an automatic electric rice cooker. Rice cookers are readily available from online retailers, in department stores, and in Indian and Asian grocery stores. Rice cookers come in various sizes, ranging from a small 4-cup size to larger sizes. Simply follow the manufacturer's instructions for perfect rice every time.

On the Stove-top:
Rinse the rice in warm water 2 to 3 times to remove starch and other residue, rubbing the rice gently with your fingers to loosen the starches. Slowly pour off the water and place rice in a saucepan. Add the indicated amount of water to the pan, and bring to a boil. Reduce heat and simmer for the indicated time. Leave the cover on and do not stir. If rice is too moist, remove the cover and continue cooking over low heat to allow the water to evaporate.

QUINOA

Hardy, nutritious quinoa makes a great substitute for rice. Interestingly, it is a member of the same food family as spinach, Swiss chard, and beets, and comes in tan, red, orange, pink, purple, and black varieties. Quinoa is gluten-free and contains all nine essential amino acids, making it a complete protein and an excellent nutritional choice. It is also rich in lysine, an amino acid that is only found in low quantities in most grains. Simple, healthy, delicious, and easy to prepare, it is available in regular and natural food stores.

BASIC COOKING INSTRUCTIONS FOR QUINOA:
To rinse quinoa, use a sieve with a fine enough mesh to trap the tiny seeds. Immerse the sieve in a big bowl of cold water until the seeds are all covered with water. Rub the seeds with your fingers to help remove the saponin. Lift the strainer with the seeds out of the water. Change the water in the bowl. Repeat 2 or 3 times until the water is clear and no foam forms on the surface.

Once the quinoa is rinsed, to 1 cup quinoa add 2 cups of water in a saucepan. Bring to a boil and then reduce the heat to simmer and cover. Cook about 15 minutes or until the germ separates from the seed. The cooked germ looks like a tiny curl and should have a slight resistance when you eat it. Remove from heat and allow to sit for 5 minutes. Fluff gently with a fork and serve.

For a nuttier taste, after rinsing try dry roasting the quinoa in a skillet for about 5 minutes before adding the water and cooking.

Bell Pepper and Tomato Rice with Cashews

[Serves 4 to 6]

 This hearty, flavorful, and nutritious rice dish can be served with any meal. It makes a colorful, splendid addition to Thanksgiving dinner.

1 cup basmati rice

1 tablespoon oil

1 tablespoon unsalted butter

2 or 3 curry leaves

2 to 4 (½-inch-long) slivers cinnamon stick

1 bay leaf

½ teaspoon cumin seeds

½ teaspoon fennel seeds

½ cup onion slices cut lengthwise

¼ cup diced tomato

1 cup coarsely chopped green bell peppers*

¼ teaspoon ground turmeric

1 teaspoon curry powder

1 teaspoon salt

¼ cup tomato sauce

¼ cup cashew halves

1 tablespoon chopped red onion

*Or use a combination of green, red, and orange bell peppers for a multi-colored pepper rice.

1 Rinse and drain rice 2 to 3 times with warm water until water runs clear. Cook rice in a rice cooker or saucepan in 2 cups of water until tender, following directions on box. Transfer cooked rice into a bowl. Fluff and let it cool for about 15 minutes, fluffing a few times so grains do not stick together.

2 Heat oil and butter in a skillet or wok over medium heat. When oil is hot, but not smoking, add cinnamon sticks, bay leaf, cumin seeds, and fennel seeds. Brown for a few seconds.

3 Add onion slices and tomato and stir-fry for 1 minute.

4 Add bell peppers, turmeric, curry powder, and salt. Mix well.

5 Stir in tomato sauce. Cook, covered, over medium heat, until bell peppers become slightly tender, approximately 1 minute, stirring occasionally. (Do not over cook the bell peppers.)

6 Add cooked rice to skillet/wok and gently stir well with sauce. Immediately reduce heat and stir in cashew halves and red onions. Fluff and mix the rice. Serve warm.

Black Pepper and Cumin Rice with Cashews

[Serves 4 to 6]

 This rice showcases the tasty, aromatic combination of black pepper and cumin. A distinctively savory rice dish that is especially good with seafood.

1 cup basmati rice

2 tablespoons oil

1 whole dried red chili pepper more or less to taste

½ teaspoon black mustard seeds

½ teaspoon urad dal

1 cup chopped yellow onions

2 teaspoons Black Pepper and Cumin Powder (page 4)

½ teaspoon salt more or less to taste

¼ cup dry roasted cashews (or any toasted nut desired)

1 tablespoon finely chopped cilantro

1 Rinse and drain rice 2 to 3 times with warm water until water runs clear. Cook basmati rice in 2 cups of warm water in a rice cooker or on stovetop (see page 79). Transfer rice to a bowl. Fluff gently to separate the grains. Reserve.

2 Heat oil in a large skillet over medium-high heat. When the oil is hot, but not smoking, add chili pepper, mustard seeds, and urad dal and stir until mustard seeds start to pop and urad dal turns golden.

3 Add onions and cook for 1 minute while stirring.

4 Add reserved cooked rice, Black Pepper and Cumin Powder, salt, and cashews and stir until blended. Garnish with fresh cilantro. Stir rice gently and serve.

Carrot Rice with Cashews

[Serves 4 to 6]

 Cashews add subtle flavor to this bright, colorful carrot rice dish. It pairs well with almost any main dish—a sure winner on the dinner table.

1 cup basmati rice

1 tablespoon unsalted butter

1 tablespoon oil

1 bay leaf

1 or 2 (½-inch-long) slivers cinnamon stick

½ teaspoon cumin seeds

½ **cup sliced onion** cut lengthwise

½ **teaspoon ground cumin**

1 teaspoon salt

1 cup shredded carrots

½ cup roasted cashew halves

1 tablespoon minced fresh cilantro

1 Rinse and drain rice 2 to 3 times with warm water until water runs clear. Cook basmati rice in 2 cups of warm water in a rice cooker or on stovetop (see page 79). Transfer cooked rice to a bowl. Fluff rice and set aside to cool.

2 Heat butter and oil over medium heat in a wide saucepan. When butter is hot, but not smoking, add bay leaf and cinnamon stick. Stir-fry for 1 minute. Add cumin seeds and stir-fry for 20 seconds.

3 Add onion slices and cook for 1 minute. Add reserved cooked rice, ground cumin, salt, and carrots. Fluff rice and carrots gently on low heat.

4 Garnish with cashews and cilantro.

VARIATION

To make **Carrot and Peas Rice with Cashews** just add ½ **cup thawed frozen peas** when you add the carrots.

Cauliflower Rice with Cashews

[Serves 4 to 6]

 Fragrant basmati rice cooked with cauliflower and red onions. This hearty rice makes a satisfying vegetarian main dish.

1 cup basmati rice

1 tablespoon oil

1 tablespoon unsalted butter

1 bay leaf

2 to 4 (½-inch-long) slivers cinnamon stick

½ teaspoon cumin seeds

1 cup chopped onions

2 cups cauliflower florets

1 teaspoon Black Pepper and Cumin Powder
(page 4; more if desired)

1 teaspoon salt

¼ cup roasted cashews

2 tablespoons chopped red onions

1 teaspoon melted butter optional

1 Rinse and drain rice 2 to 3 times with warm water until water runs clear. Cook basmati rice in 2 cups of warm water in a rice cooker or on stovetop (see page 79). Transfer the cooked rice to a bowl and fluff the rice. Set aside.

2 Put oil and butter in a wide-bottomed skillet over medium heat. When oil and butter are hot, but not smoking, add bay leaf, cinnamon sticks, and cumin seeds and stir over medium heat until cumin seeds change color, about 10 seconds.

3 Add onions and cauliflower and stir-fry for a few minutes.

4 Add Black Pepper and Cumin Powder and salt. Cover, cook over medium heat until cauliflower is crisp-tender, about 2 minutes.

5 Add cooked basmati rice. Stir well into cauliflower mixture. Cover and allow to steam over low heat until rice becomes softer and absorbs the flavor of the cauliflower. Add cashews and red onion. Fluff the rice gently.

6 Optional step: 1 teaspoon of melted butter may be added to rice mixture before serving to enhance the flavor. Mix gently.

Chickpea and Apple Rice

[Serves 4 to 6]

 Aromatic basmati rice with chickpeas, apples, and ginger makes a wholesome side dish.

½ **cup basmati rice**

1 **tablespoon oil**

1 **tablespoon unsalted butter**

1 **whole dried red chili pepper**

½ **teaspoon black mustard seeds**

½ **teaspoon urad dal**

1 **cup canned chickpeas** drained and rinsed
(more, if desired)

1 **cup peeled and finely chopped Granny
Smith apples**

2 **tablespoons grated fresh ginger**

1 **teaspoon minced fresh green chili peppers**
more if desired

1 **tablespoon fresh lemon juice**

½ **teaspoon ground turmeric**

½ **teaspoon salt** more or less to taste

1 Rinse and drain rice 2 to 3 times with warm water until water runs clear. Cook basmati rice in 1 cup of warm water in a rice cooker or on stovetop (see page 79). Transfer rice to a bowl. Fluff rice gently to separate the grains. Set aside.

2 Heat oil and butter in a skillet over medium-high heat. When the oil is hot but not smoking, add red chili pepper, mustard seeds, and urad dal; stir until mustard seeds start to pop and urad dal is golden.

3 Add cooked rice, chickpeas, apple, ginger, green chili pepper, lemon juice, turmeric, and salt. Mix well and cook over medium-low heat for 1 to 2 minutes.

Coconut Rice with Cashews

[Serves 4]

 This seasoned rice with coconut and cashews is an exquisite, festive dish!

½ cup basmati rice

1 cup fresh unsweetened shredded coconut*

2 tablespoons oil

½ teaspoon asafoetida powder

1 whole dried red chili pepper

2 to 4 curry leaves optional

1 teaspoon black mustard seeds

1 teaspoon urad dal

¼ cup roasted cashew halves

1 teaspoon salt

1 tablespoon chopped fresh cilantro

1 teaspoon coconut oil (optional)

*Fresh shredded coconut is available in Indian and Mexican grocery stores in the freezer section.

1 Rinse and drain rice 2 to 3 times with warm water until water runs clear. Cook basmati rice in 1 cup of warm water in a rice cooker or on stovetop (see page 79). Transfer cooked rice to a bowl. Fluff and set rice aside to cool.

2 Heat a non-stick skillet or wok and dry roast the shredded coconut on low heat, stirring constantly, about 2 minutes. Remove coconut from skillet/wok and set aside (this removes water content from fresh coconut).

3 Heat oil in the skillet or wok over medium heat. When oil is hot, but not smoking, add asafoetida powder, red chili pepper, curry leaves, mustard seeds, and urad dal. Cover and fry until mustard seeds pop and urad dal turns golden brown, about 30 seconds.

4 Add cooked rice and mix well. Stir in the roasted coconut and mix well. Add cashews, salt, and cilantro. Mix well.

5 Optional step: Warm 1 teaspoon coconut oil and add to the rice and gently fluff.

Fragrant Lemon Rice

[Serves 4 to 6]

 Enriched with lemon, ginger, and seasonings, this delicately flavored rice makes a delicious accompaniment to any meal. It keeps well at room temperature and can be packed for lunch.

1 cup jasmine, extra-long-grain, or basmati rice

¼ cup fresh lemon juice

1 teaspoon salt

½ teaspoon ground turmeric

2 tablespoons oil

1 whole dried red chili pepper

½ teaspoon asafoetida powder

2 to 4 curry leaves optional

1 teaspoon black mustard seeds

1 teaspoon urad dal

2 teaspoons chutney powder

½ chopped fresh green chili pepper optional

3 tablespoons grated fresh ginger

½ teaspoon grated lemon peel

¼ cup dry-roasted unsalted peanuts optional

2 tablespoons minced fresh cilantro

1 Rinse and drain rice 2 to 3 times with warm water until water runs clear. Cook basmati rice in 2 cups of warm water in a rice cooker or on stovetop (see page 79). Transfer rice to a bowl. Allow rice to cool for a few minutes. Fluff gently to separate the grains. Reserve.

2 Combine lemon juice, salt, and turmeric in a small bowl. Set aside.

3 Heat oil in a large skillet or wok over medium heat. When oil is hot, but not smoking, add red chili pepper, asafoetida powder, curry leaves, mustard seeds, and urad dal. Cover and heat until mustard seeds pop and urad dal is golden brown, about 30 seconds.

4 Immediately stir in lemon juice mixture and chutney powder. Simmer 1 minute, reducing heat if mixture starts to boil.

5 Reduce heat to low. Add cooked rice and stir gently.

6 Add green chili pepper, ginger, and lemon peel. Stir and fluff seasoned rice gently. Serve garnished with peanuts (if desired) and cilantro.

Savory Mushroom Rice

[Serves 4 to 6]

 This simply prepared rice dish can be served with vegetarian or non-vegetarian main courses. It goes well with Potato Kurma (page 199), Vegetable Kurma (page 219), or Chicken Kurma (page 233).

1 tablespoon unsalted butter

1 tablespoon oil

1 bay leaf

1 teaspoon cumin seeds

½ cup chopped onions

2 cups chopped mushrooms (portabella, cremini, etc.)

1 teaspoon Black Pepper and Cumin Powder (page 4)

½ teaspoon salt

1 cup cooked basmati rice fluffed and warm

1 Heat butter and oil in a skillet or wok. When oil is hot, but not smoking, add bay leaf and cumin seeds. Heat until cumin seeds are golden brown, about 30 seconds.

2 Add onions and sauté for a few minutes.

3 Add mushrooms and sauté for a few additional minutes over medium heat. Add Black Pepper and Cumin Powder and salt. Stir and mix over low heat.

4 Add cooked rice and blend well.

Spinach Rice with Cashews

[Serves 4 to 6]

 What could be better than fluffy basmati rice combined with a richly-seasoned spinach and lentil dish? Comfort food at its finest! This dish is an excellent accompaniment to any chicken or fish recipe, vegetable side dish, or yogurt salad.

**1½ cups cooked Spinach Poriyal with
Lentils and Coconut** (page 211)

1 cup cooked and fluffed white basmati rice

½ teaspoon ground cumin optional

¼ cup unsalted roasted cashews

1 Prepare the Spinach Poriyal with Lentils and Coconut.

2 In a skillet, combine cooked rice with spinach mixture over low to medium heat. Fluff rice gently. Add ½ teaspoon cumin, if desired.

3 Garnish rice with cashews and serve.

Seasoned Cabbage Rice Pilaf

[Serves 4]

 Here rice and seasoned cabbage are combined into a nutritious and flavorful rice dish!

3 cups cooked Cabbage with Ginger Poriyal
(page 162)

½ cup white extra-long-grain or basmati rice

1 teaspoon oil

1 teaspoon unsalted butter

¼ cup toasted cashew halves

1 teaspoon finely chopped green onions
optional

1 Prepare Cabbage with Ginger Poriyal; reserve.

2 Rinse and drain rice 2 to 3 times with warm water until water runs clear. Cook rice in 1½ cups of warm water in a rice cooker or on stovetop (see page 79). Allow cooked rice to cool for a few minutes then transfer to a bowl and fluff gently to separate the grains.

3 In a skillet, warm the oil and butter. Add the cooked rice and reserved cabbage mixture. Stir together until warmed.

4 Garnish with cashews and green onions.

Tomato Rice with Green Onions

[Serves 4 to 6]

 This easy-to-prepare fragrant rice dish may be served with Minty Cucumber Yogurt Salad (page 108), Potato Kurma (page 199), Chicken Kurma (pages 233), or any grilled or baked meat or fish.

½ cup basmati rice

1 tablespoon oil

1 tablespoon unsalted butter

1 dried bay leaf

1 or 2 (½-inch-long) slivers cinnamon stick

½ teaspoon cumin seeds

½ teaspoon fennel seeds

½ cup chopped onions

1 cup chopped tomatoes

¼ teaspoon ground turmeric

1 teaspoon curry powder

¼ cup tomato sauce

½ teaspoon salt

½ cup chopped green onion tops

¼ cup roasted cashews

1 Rinse and drain rice 2 to 3 times with warm water until water runs clear. Cook rice in 1 cup of warm water in a rice cooker or on stovetop (see page 79). Transfer cooked rice to a bowl and fluff and set aside to cool for about 10 minutes.

2 Place oil and butter in a wok or wide-bottomed skillet and heat over medium heat. When oil is hot, but not smoking, add bay leaf, cinnamon sticks, cumin seeds, and fennel seeds. Fry until cumin seeds are golden, about 30 seconds.

3 Add onions and tomatoes and sauté for a few minutes. Add turmeric, curry powder, and tomato sauce. Stir well and reduce heat to low. Continue cooking uncovered for 1 to 2 minutes.

4 Add salt and mix well. Add cooked rice and fluff into mixture. Add green onions and cashews and stir gently.

Yogurt Rice

[Serves 4]

 A cooling and satisfying yogurt rice that is traditionally served as a final course in a South Indian meal. For this dish, you want to achieve a creamy consistency so you might use a masher to soften the rice to ensure that.

1 cup cooked extra-long-grain rice or jasmine rice

2 cups plain yogurt

½ cup buttermilk optional

1 teaspoon minced fresh ginger

1 teaspoon grated fresh lemon zest

½ teaspoon salt

1 Put rice, yogurt, and buttermilk in a bowl and mix well. More yogurt may be added, if desired.

2 Add ginger, lemon zest, and salt. Mix well and serve.

Note: You can also prepare Yogurt Rice in advance, refrigerate, and serve cold.

VARIATION

To make **Savory Yogurt Rice**, after you have mixed the Yogurt Rice, place **1 teaspoon oil** in a small saucepan and heat until hot but not smoking. Add **½ teaspoon black mustard seeds** and **½ teaspoon urad dal** and cook until mustard seeds pop and urad dal is golden, about 30 seconds. Pour the mixture over the yogurt rice and mix well. Garnish with **2 tablespoons chopped fresh cilantro**.

Vegetable Quinoa

[Serves 4 to 6]

 This is an easy recipe that combines a few freezer and pantry staples to create a flavorful and nutritionally balanced vegetarian meal or side dish.

1 cup quinoa (may use red or white)

1 tablespoon oil

1 teaspoon cumin seeds

¼ cup finely chopped onions

¼ teaspoon grated fresh ginger

½ cup frozen peas and carrots thawed

2½ cups hot water

¼ teaspoon salt more or less to taste

¼ cup minced fresh cilantro

2 tablespoons chopped toasted cashews

1 To rinse quinoa: using a sieve with a fine enough mesh to trap the tiny seeds, immerse the sieve in a big bowl of cold water until the seeds are all covered with water. Rub the seeds with your fingers to help remove the saponin. Lift the strainer with the seeds out of the water. Change the water in the bowl. Repeat this step 2 or 3 times until the water is clear and no foam forms on the surface. Drain quinoa and reserve.

2 Heat oil in a 2-quart saucepan over medium-high heat. When the oil is hot but not smoking, add cumin seeds and stir until seeds change color from light brown to semi-dark brown.

3 Add onions and ginger and sauté for a few minutes over medium heat. Add the rinsed quinoa and cook for 1 minute while stirring. Add thawed peas and carrots, hot water, and salt; reduce to a simmer. Cover and cook over low heat for about 15 to 20 minutes or until all of the water is absorbed.

4 Fluff quinoa with a fork. Add cilantro and cashews; fluff with fork and serve hot.

Salads

Chickpeas with Ginger and Mango

[Serves 4]

 This warm composed salad features hearty chickpeas, tangy green mango, and a zing of ginger. It makes for a high-protein, high-fiber side dish or snack.

1 (15-ounce) can chickpeas

1 tablespoon oil

½ teaspoon black mustard seeds

½ teaspoon urad dal

¼ teaspoon ground turmeric

1 teaspoon chutney powder

1 teaspoon grated fresh ginger

¼ teaspoon salt more or less to taste

½ cup chopped fresh unripe mango

1 teaspoon grated fresh coconut or unsweetened dried coconut

1 Drain chickpeas, rinse, and reserve.

2 Heat oil in a skillet over medium-high heat. When the oil is hot but not smoking, add black mustard seeds and urad dal and stir until mustard seeds start to pop and urad dal turns golden, about 30 seconds.

3 Add chickpeas, turmeric, chutney powder, ginger, and salt. Mix well. Cook over medium-low heat covered for 1 to 2 minutes.

4 Add mango. Stir over low heat for 1 minute.

5 Add coconut and stir the mixture gently. Serve warm.

VARIATION
To make **Chickpeas with Ginger and Apple** substitute **½ cup unpeeled, diced green apple** for the mango.

Minty Cucumber Yogurt Salad

[Serves 4]

 I like to serve this refreshing, cooling salad alongside spicy dishes. You can whip it up so quickly and it makes a perfect counterbalance to hot curries or other fiery foods.

½ **cup plain low-fat yogurt**

½ **teaspoon Black Pepper and Cumin Powder** (page 4)

¼ **teaspoon salt** more or less to taste

½ **English cucumber** diced (about 2 cups)

¼ **cup minced fresh mint leaves** discard stems

1 Whisk the yogurt, Black Pepper and Cumin Powder, and salt in a bowl until smooth.

2 Mix in cucumber and mint.

3 Serve at room temperature or refrigerate 30 minutes and serve chilled.

Fruit and Yogurt Medley

[Makes 2½ cups]

 Yogurt "desserts," typically laden with fruit, nuts, and spices, are common in India. This dish tastes like a creamy treat, but is still packed with a variety of appealing fruits.

1½ cups plain low-fat yogurt

½ teaspoon sugar or stevia equivalent

½ teaspoon ground cumin

⅛ teaspoon cayenne pepper powder

½ cup halved seedless black or red grapes

½ cup halved seedless green grapes

½ firm banana sliced

1 (5-ounce) can mandarin oranges drained

¼ cup chopped walnuts

1 Whisk the yogurt, sugar or stevia, cumin, and cayenne in a bowl until smooth.

2 Reserve a few pieces of each fruit and the walnuts for garnish. Add remaining grapes, banana, oranges, and walnuts to yogurt mixture and stir gently.

3 Serve garnished with reserved fruit and nuts.

Pomegranate Yogurt Salad

[Serves 4]

 Pomegranate seeds, called arils, are rich in fiber, vitamins, and phytochemicals. These ruby red gems add crunch and tang to yogurt. A vibrant side salad!

¾ **cup plain low-fat yogurt**
¼ **teaspoon ground cumin**
¼ **teaspoon salt**
¼ **cup chopped red onion**
1 **cup pomegranate seeds**
Chopped pistachios for garnish optional

1 Whisk yogurt, cumin, and salt until smooth.

2 Stir in onion and pomegranate seeds, reserving a few seeds for garnish.

3 Serve topped with reserved pomegranate seeds and pistachios.

Seasoned Vegetable Yogurt Salad

[Serves 4]

 Refreshing and easy-to-make, this colorful salad is a perfect way to enjoy your garden's summer bounty. It is an excellent accompaniment to any meal.

1 cup diced English cucumbers
½ cup diced zucchini
½ cup diced yellow summer squash
½ cup diced tomato
1½ cups plain low-fat yogurt
1 teaspoon ground cumin
¼ **teaspoon salt** more or less to taste

1 Place all the vegetables in a serving bowl.

2 In a small bowl, whisk yogurt, cumin, and salt until smooth.

3 Pour yogurt mixture over diced vegetables and stir to coat. Taste and add additional seasonings if desired.

4 Serve immediately or refrigerate and serve chilled.

Seasoned Tomato Yogurt Salad

[Serves 4]

 Simple ingredients yield complex flavors in this salad. It is a perfect way to enjoy summer onions and tomatoes, and a refreshing accompaniment to almost any dish.

1 teaspoon oil

1 whole dried red chili pepper

½ teaspoon black mustard seeds

½ teaspoon urad dal

1 cup chopped onions

1 cup chopped tomatoes

¼ teaspoon ground turmeric

½ teaspoon cayenne pepper powder

2 cups plain yogurt

1 teaspoon salt

2 tablespoons chopped fresh cilantro leaves

1 Place oil in a saucepan over medium heat. When oil is hot, but not smoking, add red chili pepper, mustard seeds, and urad dal. Cook, covered, until mustard seeds pop and urad dal is golden brown, about 30 seconds.

2 Add onions and tomatoes. Stir-fry for a few minutes. Add turmeric and cayenne and cook for a few more minutes.

3 Transfer ingredients from saucepan to a bowl and allow to cool.

4 Stir yogurt into cooled tomato mixture. Add salt and stir. Garnish with cilantro leaves.

Sambhars & Kulambus

WHAT IS SAMBHAR?

Vegetables and dals (lentils) cooked with sambhar powder (a spice blend that is readily available) to make a hearty sauce with a medium-thick consistency. There are a wide variety of sambhars prepared with an array of vegetables. You can serve sambhars over rice or other grains or with breakfast items.

WHAT IS KULAMBU?

A thick vegetable sauce usually made without dals (lentils). Kulambu features numerous individual vegetables, and occasionally meats, cooked with tamarind paste and a variety of spices.

DALS

Dals are very easy to cook. In each recipe where dals are used, I provide easy-to-follow stovetop cooking instructions. Pressure cookers are used often in Indian households to cook all types of legumes.

(See pages 6-7 for a description of the dals used in the recipes in this book.)

Bell Pepper and Radish Sambhar

[Serves 4]

 In this recipe, bell peppers and radishes are cooked with spices in a creamy lentil base. This sambhar is best served over plain rice, but can also be served as soup with bread.

½ cup masoor dal (red lentils)

½ teaspoon ground turmeric divided

2 tablespoons oil

¼ teaspoon asafoetida powder

1 whole dried red chili pepper

½ teaspoon fenugreek seeds

1 teaspoon black mustard seeds

1 teaspoon urad dal

½ cup chopped onions

½ cup coarsely chopped tomatoes

1 cup thinly sliced white or red radishes

½ teaspoon tamarind paste

2 teaspoons sambhar powder

1½ teaspoons salt

1 cup tomato sauce

2 cups coarsely chopped green bell peppers

1 tablespoon chopped fresh cilantro leaves

1 Bring 3 cups of water to a boil in a deep saucepan. Add masoor dal and ¼ teaspoon turmeric. Reduce heat to medium and cook, uncovered, for about 30 minutes until dal becomes creamy (if water evaporates during the cooking process, add another cup of water). Set aside.

2 Put oil in a saucepan over medium heat. When the oil is hot, but not smoking, add asafoetida powder, red chili pepper, fenugreek seeds, mustard seeds, and urad dal. Cook, covered, until mustard seeds pop and other ingredients are golden brown, about 15 seconds.

3 Add the onions and tomatoes and cook for 1 minute. Add the remaining ¼ teaspoon turmeric and radishes. Cook over medium heat, stirring constantly, for 1 minute.

4 Add the creamy dal mixture and 2 cups of water. Add the tamarind paste, sambhar powder, and salt. Cover and cook over low heat for 10 minutes.

5 Add tomato sauce. When the mixture begins to boil add green bell peppers. Cover and cook over low heat for 2 to 3 minutes. (Do not overcook the green peppers.) Add fresh cilantro and serve.

Note: If the finished sambhar is too thick, add an additional ½ to 1 cup of warm water.

Brussels Sprouts Kulambu

[Serves 4]

 The slightly bitter flavor of Brussels sprouts is balanced by sweet and sour tamarind in this vegetable dish. This saucy dish is best served over plain rice or as a side dish. It makes a flavorful addition to the Thanksgiving table too!

2 cups fresh Brussels sprouts cut in half (if large, cut in quarters so all about same size)

2 tablespoons oil

¼ teaspoon asafoetida powder

2 to 4 curry leaves optional

½ teaspoon fenugreek seeds

½ teaspoon black mustard seeds

½ teaspoon urad dal

½ cup chopped onions

½ cup chopped tomatoes

4 garlic cloves quartered

¼ teaspoon ground turmeric

3 teaspoons sambhar powder

1 cup tomato sauce

¼ teaspoon tamarind paste optional

1 teaspoon salt

1 Place cut Brussels sprouts in a steamer and steam for about 3 to 4 minutes until crisp tender. Set aside.

2 Place oil in a saucepan over medium heat. When the oil is hot, but not smoking, add asafoetida powder, curry leaves, fenugreek seeds, mustard seeds, and urad dal. Cover and cook over medium heat until the mustard seeds pop and urad dal is golden brown, about 15 seconds.

3 Add onions, tomatoes, garlic, and turmeric. Stir for 1 minute. Add steamed Brussels sprouts and stir with spices to coat.

4 Add sambhar powder, tomato sauce, tamarind paste, and salt. Stir well. Add 2 cups of warm water to saucepan. Stir and cook for about 5 minutes.

5 Cover and cook over low heat until Brussels sprouts are just tender, about 10 minutes. Be careful not to overcook.

Carrot Sambhar

[Serves 4]

 Carrots cooked with spices in a lentil base, this sambhar is delicious served over plain rice and with idlis (page 73), dosais (page 65), chappatis, or naan bread.

½ cup masoor dal (red lentils)

½ teaspoon ground turmeric divided

2 tablespoons oil

1 whole dried red chili pepper

¼ teaspoon asafoetida powder

2 to 4 curry leaves optional

¼ teaspoon fenugreek seeds

½ teaspoon black mustard seeds

½ teaspoon urad dal

½ cup chopped onions

¼ cup chopped tomatoes

1 cup peeled and thinly sliced fresh carrots

2 teaspoons sambhar powder

¼ teaspoon tamarind paste

½ cup tomato sauce

1 teaspoon salt more, if desired

1 tablespoon chopped fresh cilantro leaves

1 Bring 3 cups of water to a boil in a deep saucepan. Add masoor dal and ¼ teaspoon turmeric. Reduce heat to medium and cook, uncovered, for about 20 minutes until dal becomes creamy (if water evaporates during the cooking process, add another cup). Set aside.

2 Place oil in a large saucepan over medium heat. When oil is hot, but not smoking, add whole red chili pepper, asafoetida powder, curry leaves, fenugreek seeds, mustard seeds, and urad dal. Cook, covered, until mustard seeds pop and other ingredients are golden brown, about 15 seconds.

3 Add onions, tomatoes, and remaining ¼ teaspoon turmeric and stir-fry for 1 to 2 minutes. Add carrots and stir-fry for 1 minute.

4 Add sambhar powder, tamarind paste, tomato sauce, and salt. Cook, covered, over medium-low heat for 3 minutes, stirring occasionally.

5 Add cooked dal and 2 cups of warm water, and stir. Add cilantro. Cook, covered, over medium-low heat for another 3 to 5 minutes, until carrots are tender.

VARIATIONS
Carrot & Green Bean Sambhar or **Carrot & Zucchini Sambhar** are also great combinations. Use ½ cup of each vegetable.

Eggplant Pulikulambu

[Serves 4]

 Eggplant in tamarind sauce is a delicious Chettinad speciality. Simple eggplant becomes sublime when it is enhanced with aromatic spices. Thai eggplant (green in color) or baby eggplant is particularly delicious in this recipe. You need to remove the stems and cut the baby eggplants in quarters making the pieces all the same size.

3 tablespoons oil

1 whole dried red chili pepper

2 to 4 curry leaves optional

¼ teaspoon asafoetida powder

½ teaspoon fenugreek seeds

½ teaspoon black mustard seeds

½ teaspoon urad dal

½ cup chopped onions

½ cup chopped tomatoes

2 cups chopped unpeeled eggplant

¼ teaspoon ground turmeric

2 teaspoons sambhar powder

1 teaspoon salt

1 cup tomato sauce

½ teaspoon tamarind paste

1 Place oil in a saucepan over medium heat. When oil is hot, but not smoking, add red chili pepper, curry leaves, asafoetida powder, fenugreek seeds, mustard seeds, and urad dal. Cook spices for about 15 seconds until mustard seeds pop and urad dal becomes golden.

2 Add onions and tomatoes and sauté for 1 minute. Add eggplant and stir-fry for 2 minutes over low heat.

3 Add turmeric, sambhar powder, and salt. Stir the seasonings into the mixture over medium heat. Add tomato sauce, tamarind paste, and 1½ cups of warm water. Stir the ingredients well in saucepan.

4 Cook, covered, over low heat until eggplant becomes soft and blends well with other ingredients in the saucepan to become a delicious thickened eggplant sauce.

Garlic Kulambu

[Serves 4]

 A perfect dish for garlic lovers! When it is slow-cooked with onions, tomatoes, and spices in tamarind sauce, garlic loses its sharp pungency, becoming soft and slightly sweet in flavor. Garlic Kulambu is wonderful served over plain rice and also goes well with any Indian breads.

3 tablespoons oil

¼ teaspoon asafoetida powder

2 to 4 curry leaves optional

½ teaspoon fenugreek seeds

½ teaspoon black mustard seeds

½ teaspoon urad dal

½ cup chopped onions

½ cup chopped tomatoes

½ cup whole peeled garlic cloves

½ teaspoon ground turmeric

2 teaspoons sambhar powder

¼ teaspoon tamarind paste

½ teaspoon salt more, if desired

1 cup tomato sauce

1 tablespoon minced fresh cilantro leaves

1 Place oil in a saucepan over medium heat. When oil is hot, but not smoking, add asafoetida powder, curry leaves, fenugreek seeds, mustard seeds, and urad dal. Stir quickly and cover. Fry until mustard seeds pop and urad dal is golden, about 15 seconds.

2 Add onions, tomatoes, and garlic. Stir-fry for 1 minute. Add turmeric and mix well. Cook, covered, over medium-low heat, for about 3 minutes, until onions are tender.

3 Add sambhar powder, tamarind paste, and salt. Mix all the ingredients thoroughly while cooking over medium heat.

4 Add tomato sauce, cilantro, and 1 cup of warm water. Continue to cook, covered, until garlic is tender. The cooking time will vary with the size of the garlic cloves, about 4 to 6 minutes.

Green Beans Sambhar

[Serves 4]

 Green beans are combined with tomatoes and spices in a creamy lentil base. Green Beans Sambhar is delicious served over plain rice or with idlis (page 73), dosais (page 65), or toasted bread.

½ **cup masoor dal (red lentils)**
½ **teaspoon ground turmeric** divided
1 **cup fresh green beans**
2 **tablespoons oil**
¼ **teaspoon asafoetida powder**
2 to 4 **curry leaves**
1 **whole dried red chili pepper**
½ **teaspoon black mustard seeds**
½ **teaspoon urad dal**
½ **cup onion slices** cut lengthwise
½ **cup chopped tomatoes**
1 **teaspoon sambhar powder**
½ **teaspoon salt** more if desired
¼ **teaspoon tamarind paste**
¼ **cup tomato sauce**
1 **tablespoon chopped fresh cilantro leaves**

1 Bring 3 cups of water to a boil in a deep saucepan. Add masoor dal and ¼ teaspoon turmeric. Reduce heat to medium and cook, uncovered, for about 20 minutes, until dal becomes soft and creamy (if water evaporates during the cooking process, add another cup). Set aside.

2 Wash the green beans and cut off the ends. Cut each bean in half. Place in a bowl and set aside.

3 Heat oil in a saucepan over medium heat. When oil is hot, but not smoking, add asafoetida powder, curry leaves, red chili pepper, mustard seeds, and urad dal. Cover and cook until mustard seeds pop and urad dal turns golden brown, about 30 seconds.

4 Add onions, tomatoes, and green beans and cook for 1 minute.

5 Add remaining ¼ teaspoon turmeric, sambhar powder, and salt. Toss the seasonings well with the vegetables.

6 Add the cooked creamy dal, tamarind paste, and tomato sauce. Add 1 to 2 cups of warm water. (Sambhar can be thick or thin in consistency according to your taste, adjust the amount of water as you desire.) Stir and let mixture come to a boil.

7 Add cilantro and let mixture simmer for a few more minutes.

Kohlrabi Sambhar

[Serves 4]

 Kohlrabi is an overlooked vegetable, but paired with lentils as in this recipe it is light, flavorful, and easy to prepare. This sambhar is delicious served over plain rice and with uppuma (page 63), idlis (page 73), dosais (page 65), or any Indian breads.

½ cup masoor dal (red lentils)
½ teaspoon ground turmeric divided
2 tablespoons oil
¼ teaspoon asafoetida powder
1 whole dried red chili pepper
½ teaspoon fenugreek seeds
½ teaspoon black mustard seeds
½ teaspoon urad dal
¼ cup chopped onions
½ cup chopped tomatoes
1 cup peeled and thinly sliced kohlrabi
1 teaspoon sambhar powder
¼ cup tomato sauce
¼ teaspoon tamarind paste
1 teaspoon salt
1 tablespoon chopped fresh cilantro leaves

1 Bring 3 cups of water to a boil in a deep saucepan. Add masoor dal and ¼ teaspoon turmeric. Reduce heat to medium and cook, uncovered, for about 20 minutes, until dal becomes creamy (if water evaporates during the cooking process, add another cup). Set aside.

2 In another saucepan, heat oil over medium heat. When oil is hot, but not smoking, add asafoetida powder, whole red chili pepper, fenugreek seeds, mustard seeds, and urad dal. Cook covered, until mustard seeds pop and urad dal is golden brown, about 30 seconds.

3 Stir in onions and tomatoes and cook 2 to 3 minutes, until onions are tender. Add kohlrabi and the remaining ¼ teaspoon turmeric. Stir well.

4 Add sambhar powder and tomato sauce. Stir and then add creamy dal mixture plus 2 cups of warm water. Stir well.

5 Add tamarind paste and salt. When mixture begins to bubble, reduce heat and cook kohlrabi until tender, 3 to 5 minutes.

6 Add cilantro and simmer for an additional few minutes.

Black-eyed Peas Kulambu

[Serves 4]

 This kulambu brings many textures and flavors together beautifully: hearty black-eyed peas and tart mango in an aromatic, delicious sauce. You can serve these black-eyed peas over rice or quinoa or enjoy this kulambu on its own as a nutritious soup.

2 tablespoons oil

¼ teaspoon asafoetida powder

1 whole dried red chili pepper

¼ teaspoon fenugreek seeds

½ teaspoon black mustard seeds

½ teaspoon urad dal

1 cup onion slices cut lengthwise

½ cup chopped tomatoes

¼ teaspoon ground turmeric

2 cups frozen black-eyed peas defrosted,
   or canned black-eyed peas rinsed and
   drained

2 teaspoons sambhar powder

½ teaspoon salt

1 cup tomato sauce

2 garlic cloves crushed

1 cup peeled and cubed un-ripe fresh
   mango cut into small cubes

1 tablespoon chopped fresh cilantro leaves

1 Place oil in a warmed saucepan. When oil is hot but not smoking, add asafoetida powder, red chili pepper, fenugreek seeds, mustard seeds, and urad dal. Stir over medium heat until mustard seeds pop and urad dal is golden brown, about 30 seconds.

2 Add onions and tomatoes and stir well. Add turmeric and cook until onions are translucent.

3 Add black-eyed peas, sambhar powder, and salt and stir. Add tomato sauce and 3 cups of warm water. When mixture begins to boil, add the crushed garlic and mango. Let simmer over low heat until black-eyed peas are tender.

4 Add chopped cilantro. Serve warm.

Okra Sambhar

[Serves 4]

Okra is a favorite vegetable in Indian cooking. It's also been traditionally enjoyed in the American south and is gaining in popularity across the country now. Okra are usually abundant in the summer but harder to find in winter months. When selecting okra choose tender okra and not the tough fibrous variety. You can use frozen okra for this recipe if you can't find fresh. The okra are cooked with tomatoes and onions in a seasoned lentil sauce. This delicious sambhar is best served over plain rice.

½ **cup masoor dal (red lentils)**

½ **teaspoon ground turmeric** divided

2 **tablespoons oil**

½ **teaspoon asafoetida powder**

1 **whole dried red chili pepper**

2 **to 4 curry leaves** optional

¼ **teaspoon fenugreek seeds**

½ **teaspoon black mustard seeds**

½ **teaspoon urad dal**

½ **cup chopped onions**

¼ **cup chopped tomatoes**

2 **cups okra** with tips removed and sliced into ½-inch pieces

2 **teaspoons sambhar powder**

¼ **teaspoon tamarind paste**

½ **cup tomato sauce**

1 **teaspoon salt**

1 Bring 3 cups of water to a boil in a deep saucepan over medium heat. Add masoor dal and ¼ teaspoon turmeric. Reduce heat to medium and cook, uncovered, for about 20 minutes, until dal becomes creamy (if water evaporates during the cooking process, you may add another cup). Set aside.

2 Put oil in a saucepan, and put over medium heat. When oil is hot, but not smoking, add asafoetida powder, red chili pepper, curry leaves, fenugreek seeds, mustard seeds, and urad dal. Cover and cook over medium heat until mustard seeds pop and urad dal is golden brown, about 30 seconds.

3 Add onions and tomatoes and stir well. Add okra and the remaining ¼ teaspoon turmeric and sauté for 2 to 3 minutes over medium heat.

4 Add sambhar powder, tamarind paste, tomato sauce, and salt. Stir well.

5 Add cooked dal and about 2 cups of water and stir the mixture well. Let okra continue to cook over medium-low heat for 3 to 5 minutes.

Pearl Onion and Tomato Sambhar

[Serves 4]

 This aromatic sambhar is a popular and traditional dish in South India. It is usually served over plain rice with any vegetable kootu, poriyal, or pappad. It can also be served with idlis (page 73) and dosais (page 65) during breakfast.

½ **cup masoor dal (red lentils)**

½ **teaspoon ground turmeric** divided

2 **tablespoons oil**

½ **teaspoon asafoetida powder**

2 **to 4 curry leaves**

1 **whole dried red chili pepper**

¼ **teaspoon fenugreek seeds**

½ **teaspoon black mustard seeds**

½ **teaspoon urad dal**

½ **cup (about 12) fresh pearl onions** peeled

1 **cup chopped tomatoes**

2 **teaspoons sambhar powder**

1 **teaspoon salt**

½ **cup tomato sauce**

¼ **teaspoon tamarind paste**

1 **tablespoon chopped fresh cilantro leaves**

1 Bring 3 cups of water to a boil in a deep saucepan. Add masoor dal and ¼ teaspoon turmeric. Reduce heat to medium and cook, uncovered, for about 20 minutes, until dal becomes creamy (if the water evaporates during the cooking process, add another cup). Set aside.

2 Place oil in a saucepan and heat over medium heat. When the oil is hot, but not smoking, add asafoetida powder, curry leaves, red chili pepper, fenugreek seeds, mustard seeds, and urad dal. Cook, covered, until mustard seeds pop and urad dal turns golden brown, about 30 seconds.

3 Add pearl onions and tomatoes and cover and cook for about 2 minutes, until onions are tender.

4 Add remaining ¼ teaspoon turmeric, sambhar powder, and salt and stir well with the onions and tomatoes. Cook for 1 minute.

5 Stir in tomato sauce, tamarind paste, cilantro, and 1 cup of warm water. Let onions cook in sauce over low heat, covered, for about 3 minutes.

6 Add the cooked dal and about 2 cups of warm water (making it the consistency you like). Cover and cook for 2 minutes. Stir well and serve.

Zucchini Sambhar

[Serves 4]

 This sambhar is delicious served over plain rice or with uppuma (page 63), idlis (page 73), dosais (page 65), or any Indian breads.

½ cup masoor dal (red lentils)

½ teaspoon ground turmeric divided

2 tablespoons oil

½ teaspoon asafoetida powder

1 whole dried red chili pepper

½ teaspoon fenugreek seeds

½ teaspoon black mustard seeds

½ teaspoon urad dal

½ cup onion slices cut lengthwise

½ cup chopped tomatoes

2 teaspoons sambhar powder

2 cups peeled and cubed zucchini

¼ cup tomato sauce

¼ teaspoon tamarind paste

1 teaspoon salt more, if desired

1 tablespoon chopped fresh cilantro leaves

1 Bring 3 cups of water to a boil in a deep saucepan. Add masoor dal and ¼ teaspoon turmeric. Reduce heat to medium and cook, uncovered, for about 20 minutes, until dal becomes creamy (if water evaporates during the cooking process, add another cup). Set aside.

2 In another saucepan, heat oil over medium heat. When oil is hot, but not smoking, add asafoetida powder, red chili pepper, fenugreek seeds, mustard seeds, and urad dal. Cook, covered, until mustard seeds pop and urad dal is golden brown, about 30 seconds.

3 Add onions and tomatoes and cook 2 to 3 minutes, until onions are tender. Add remaining ¼ teaspoon turmeric and the sambhar powder and stir well.

4 Add zucchini and stir. Add cooked dal, tomato sauce, tamarind paste, and salt. When mixture begins to bubble, add 1½ cups of warm water. Stir, cover, and cook over low heat until zucchini is crisp-tender.

5 Add cilantro and simmer for an additional few minutes.

Vegetable Dishes

Asparagus with Ginger and Coconut

[Serves 4]

 This recipe combines a favorite spring vegetable with ginger, coconut, and spices. The crisp, green asparagus makes a lovely presentation with the red onion and coconut.

1 teaspoon oil

½ teaspoon black mustard seeds

½ teaspoon cumin seeds

¼ cup chopped red onions

½ tablespoon grated fresh ginger

1 teaspoon minced garlic cloves

1 pound asparagus sliced diagonally into about 1½-inch pieces (about 3 cups)

½ teaspoon ground cumin

¼ teaspoon salt more or less to taste

½ tablespoon grated fresh coconut or unsweetened dried coconut

1 Heat oil in a skillet over medium-high heat. When the oil is hot but not smoking, add mustard seeds and cumin seeds and stir until mustard seeds start to pop and cumin seeds change color from light brown to semi-dark brown, about 30 seconds.

2 Stir in onions, ginger, and garlic. Add asparagus and cook for 1 minute while stirring.

3 Stir in ground cumin and salt; cover and cook 3 to 5 minutes or until asparagus is tender but still crisp.

4 Add coconut, stir, and serve.

Beets with Coconut Poriyal

[Serves 4]

 Vibrant in color and packed with vitamins, beets are a nutritional powerhouse. This recipe gives you a unique way to prepare them as a delicious side dish with spices and coconut.

3 cups washed, peeled, and cubed beets

2 tablespoons oil

1 whole dried red chili pepper

1 teaspoon mustard seeds

1 teaspoon urad dal

1 teaspoon chutney powder

½ teaspoon salt

1 tablespoon grated fresh coconut or
    unsweetened shredded coconut

1 Steam cubed beets in a steamer basket until they are tender. Set aside.

2 Heat oil in a skillet over medium-high heat. When the oil is hot, but not smoking, stir in red chili pepper, mustard seeds, and urad dal. Cover and cook until mustard seeds pop and urad dal is golden brown, about 30 seconds.

3 Add steamed beets to skillet along with chutney powder and salt. Stir well. Cook covered on low heat for 2 to 3 minutes.

4 Add coconut and mix gently.

Bell Pepper and Tomato Pachadi

[Serves 4]

 Green bell peppers are cooked in a delicious lentil sauce with onions and tomatoes. This vegetable dish can be enjoyed with rice, bread, or as a side.

¼ cup masoor dal (red lentils) or **moong dal (split yellow mung beans)**

½ teaspoon ground turmeric divided

2 tablespoons oil

1 whole dried red chili pepper

4 to 6 curry leaves

¼ teaspoon asafoetida powder optional

½ teaspoon black mustard seeds

½ teaspoon urad dal

¼ cup chopped onions

¾ cup chopped tomatoes

2 cups diced green bell peppers

½ teaspoon cayenne pepper powder

½ teaspoon ground cumin

¼ teaspoon tamarind paste optional

½ teaspoon salt

¼ cup tomato sauce

1 Bring about 2 cups of water to a boil in a saucepan. Add dal and ¼ teaspoon turmeric and cook for about 20 minutes over medium heat, uncovered, until dal is semi-soft. Set aside.

2 Heat oil in another saucepan over medium heat. When oil is hot, but not smoking, add red chili pepper, curry leaves, asafoetida powder, mustard seeds, and urad dal. Cover and fry over medium heat until mustard seeds pop and urad dal is golden brown, about 30 seconds.

3 Add onions, tomatoes, and remaining ¼ teaspoon turmeric and stir for a few minutes.

4 Add green bell peppers, cayenne, cumin, tamarind paste, and salt. Stir well. Add cooked dal, tomato sauce, and about ½ cup of warm water. Stir well. Cover and cook over medium heat until green peppers are tender.

Broccoli with Coconut Poriyal

[Serves 4]

 This is a South Indian twist on the usual broccoli stir-fry. Even if you're not fond of this vegetable, give this recipe a try—the flavors of chutney powder, mustard seeds, and coconut are sure to change your mind. It is an excellent nutritious side dish with any meal.

2 tablespoons oil

½ teaspoon black mustard seeds

1 teaspoon urad dal

¾ cup chopped onions

4 cups coarsely chopped broccoli including tender stems

1 teaspoon salt

1 teaspoon chutney powder

½ cup ground fresh coconut or unsweetened shredded coconut

1 Heat oil in a large skillet over medium heat. When oil is hot but not smoking, stir in mustard seeds and urad dal. Cover and heat until mustard seeds pop and urad dal is golden brown, about 30 seconds.

2 Add onions and stir-fry for 30 seconds.

3 Add broccoli, salt, and chutney powder and stir well. Cover and cook for 5 to 7 minutes.

4 When the broccoli is tender but still crisp, add the coconut, stir well, and serve.

Roasted Brussels Sprouts

[Serves 4]

 This roasting technique may just become your favorite way to prepare Brussels sprouts. The outer leaves will crisp and caramelize and the results are absolutely delicious.

2 tablespoons olive oil

¼ teaspoon ground cumin

¾ teaspoon garam masala

½ teaspoon salt more or less to taste

2 cups (½ pound) Brussels sprouts washed, dried, and cut in half

1 Preheat oven to 425°F.

2 In a large bowl combine oil, cumin, garam masala, and salt. Add Brussels sprouts and toss until spices and oil are evenly distributed.

3 Place the seasoned Brussels sprouts cut side down in a single layer on a dark, shallow baking sheet (do not use a light-colored pan or aluminum foil because they do not allow vegetables to brown as quickly).

4 Place in oven and roast about 15 minutes. Check if they are starting to brown on bottom. If not, return to oven for 5 minutes, or until as soft as you like. (This will vary based on your individual oven.) Serve immediately.

Brussels Sprout and Chickpea Poriyal

[Serves 4]

 A hearty and fiber-rich stir-fry dish, Brussels Sprout and Chickpea Poriyal can be served as a salad, as a side dish with any meal, or it can be enjoyed as a delicious snack!

2 tablespoons oil

1 whole dried red chili pepper

½ teaspoon black mustard seeds

½ teaspoon urad dal

½ cup chopped onions

1 can (15 ounces) chickpeas rinsed and drained

3 cups coarsely chopped fresh Brussels sprouts

1 teaspoon salt

1 teaspoon chutney powder

½ cup ground fresh coconut or unsweetened shredded coconut

1 Heat oil in a skillet over medium heat. When oil is hot, but not smoking, stir in red chili pepper, mustard seeds, and urad dal. Cover and fry until mustard seeds pop and urad dal is golden brown, about 30 seconds.

2 Add onions and stir for 30 seconds. Add drained chickpeas. Stir, cover, and cook for about 2 minutes.

3 Add chopped Brussels sprouts, salt, and chutney powder and stir well. Cover and cook for 2 minutes over medium heat (be careful not to overcook the Brussels sprouts).

4 Add coconut. Mix well and cook for an additional minute.

VARIATION
Use chopped Brussels sprouts without chickpeas to prepare just **Brussels Sprout Poriyal**.

Brussels Sprouts Masala

[Serves 4]

 Brussels sprouts cooked with tomatoes and seasonings make a delicious accompaniment to any meal. This is a flavorful option for those who like their vegetables with a little kick!

2 cups quartered Brussels sprouts

2 tablespoons oil

½ teaspoon black mustard seeds

½ teaspoon urad dal

½ cup chopped onions

1 cup chopped tomatoes

¼ teaspoon ground turmeric

½ teaspoon cayenne pepper powder more, if desired

½ teaspoon ground cumin

½ teaspoon salt

½ cup tomato sauce

1 teaspoon unsweetened shredded coconut

1 Steam Brussels sprouts until crisp tender. Set aside.

2 Place oil in a saucepan over medium heat. When oil is hot, but not smoking, add mustard seeds and urad dal and cover and fry until mustard seeds pop and urad dal turns golden, about 30 seconds.

3 Add onions, tomatoes, and turmeric and cook until onions are tender.

4 Add cayenne, cumin, and salt. Cook for 1 minute. Add tomato sauce and stir well.

5 Add steamed Brussels sprouts and coat sprouts well with seasonings. Cover and cook over medium-low heat until Brussels sprouts are tender.

6 Add coconut and mix well.

Butternut Squash Masala

[Serves 4]

 What's not to like about butternut squash? It's packed with vitamins A and C, is rich in dietary fiber, and is delicious too. This winter squash is popular on holiday tables, and this recipe offers a tasty way to enjoy it with spices and coconut.

2 teaspoons oil

1 teaspoon black mustard seeds

½ teaspoon cumin seeds

½ **medium onion** sliced lengthwise (about ½ cup)

½ cup chopped tomatoes

½ teaspoon ground turmeric

½ **teaspoon cayenne pepper powder** more or less to taste

½ teaspoon ground cumin

¼ **teaspoon salt** more or less to taste

¼ cup tomato sauce

1 **pound butternut squash** peeled and cut in 1-inch cubes (about 2 cups)*

2 **tablespoons grated fresh coconut** or unsweetened dried coconut

2 tablespoons chopped fresh cilantro

1 Heat oil in a skillet over medium-high heat. When the oil is hot but not smoking, add mustard seeds and cumin seeds and stir until mustard seeds start to pop, about 30 seconds.

2 Add onion and tomatoes and cook for 1 minute while stirring.

3 Add turmeric, cayenne, ground cumin, salt, and tomato sauce; stir and bring to a boil.

4 Add butternut squash, cover, and cook over medium heat for 5 to 7 minutes or until tender when pierced with a fork, adding water a tablespoon at a time if needed.

5 Add coconut and cilantro, gently stir and serve warm.

*Peeled pre-cut squash is available in some grocery stores.

Spiced Spaghetti Squash

[Serves 4]

 Strands of spaghetti squash tossed with sautéed mustard seeds and cumin seeds and fragrant flavor-enhancing garam masala makes a unique, tasty side dish.

1 (3-pound) spaghetti squash (4 cups cooked)

1 tablespoon oil

1 teaspoon black mustard seeds

1 teaspoon cumin seeds

½ cup chopped onions

½ fresh green chili pepper minced (more or less to taste)

½ teaspoon garam masala

¼ teaspoon salt more or less to taste

¼ cup chopped fresh cilantro

2 small whole dried red chili peppers optional for garnish

1 To cook squash in microwave, cut in half lengthwise and remove seeds. Place cut side down in microwave and cook on high for 10 to 12 minutes or until soft. Let cool slightly.

2 Using a fork, pull the flesh lengthwise to separate it into long strands until you have 4 cups of squash. Save any additional squash for another time or freeze.

3 Heat oil in a skillet over medium-high heat. When the oil is hot but not smoking, add mustard seeds and cumin seeds and stir until mustard seeds start to pop and cumin seeds change color from light brown to semi-dark brown, about 30 seconds.

4 Add onions, chili pepper, garam masala, and salt. Sauté for 2 to 3 minutes until onions are tender. Add squash and toss to coat with the seasonings.

5 Place in serving dish and garnish with cilantro and red chili peppers, if using.

Cabbage Kootu

[Serves 4]

 Kootu is a thick, lightly seasoned vegetable dish (in this case using cabbage) cooked with ginger and lentils. Serve as a side for any meal.

¾ **cup masoor dal (red lentils)**

½ **teaspoon ground turmeric** divided

2 **tablespoons oil**

2 or 3 **curry leaves** optional

½ **teaspoon black mustard seeds**

½ **teaspoon urad dal**

½ **cup chopped onions**

1 **fresh green chili pepper** minced (more, if desired)

1 **tablespoon minced fresh ginger**

2 **cups coarsely shredded cabbage**

1 **teaspoon ground cumin**

1 **teaspoon salt**

1 Bring 3 cups of water to a boil in a deep saucepan. Add masoor dal and ¼ teaspoon turmeric. Reduce heat to medium and cook dal, uncovered, until it becomes soft and tender, about 20 minutes (if most of the water evaporates before dal becomes soft, add an additional cup). Set aside.

2 Heat oil in a saucepan over medium heat. When oil is hot, but not smoking, add curry leaves, mustard seeds, and urad dal. Cover and cook until mustard seeds pop and urad dal is golden brown, about 30 seconds.

3 Add onions, chili pepper, and ginger. Stir well. Add cabbage and stir-fry about 1 minute.

4 Add remaining ¼ teaspoon turmeric, cumin, and salt and stir well. Immediately add cooked dal and about 1 cup of water. Cover and cook over medium heat for 5 to 7 minutes, stirring frequently so that cabbage is cooked and tender.

VARIATION

To make **Cabbage and Carrot Kootu** use **1 cup shredded carrots** in place of one of the cups of cabbage.

Cabbage and Carrot Poriyal

[Serves 4]

 Shredded cabbage, carrots, green chili peppers, ginger, and coconut come together in this colorful, flavorful, and healthy side dish.

2 tablespoons oil

2 to 4 curry leaves optional

1 whole dried red chili pepper

½ teaspoon black mustard seeds

½ teaspoon urad dal

3 cups shredded cabbage

½ cup shredded carrots

½ fresh green chili pepper chopped

½ teaspoon minced fresh ginger

½ teaspoon salt more, if desired

1 tablespoon unsweetened shredded coconut

1 Place oil in a skillet over medium heat. When oil is hot, but not smoking, stir in curry leaves, red chili pepper, mustard seeds, and urad dal. Cover and fry until mustard seeds pop and urad dal is golden brown, about 30 seconds.

2 Add cabbage and carrots. Stir well and then stir in green chili pepper, ginger, and salt. Cover and cook over low heat until cabbage is crisp tender, about 2 to 3 minutes.

3 Add shredded coconut and stir well.

Cabbage with Ginger Poriyal

[Serves 4]

 A stir-fry cabbage dish with ginger and coconut, this cabbage poriyal is a crisp-tender, delicious side dish!

2 tablespoons oil

2 to 4 curry leaves optional

½ teaspoon black mustard seeds

½ teaspoon urad dal

3 cups shredded cabbage

1 teaspoon minced fresh ginger

½ fresh green chili pepper chopped

½ teaspoon salt more, if desired

1 tablespoon ground fresh coconut or unsweetened shredded coconut

1 Heat oil in a skillet over medium heat. When oil is hot, but not smoking, stir in curry leaves, mustard seeds, and urad dal. Cover and fry until mustard seeds pop and urad dal is golden brown, about 30 seconds.

2 Add cabbage, ginger, and green chili pepper. Stir well and add salt. Cover and cook over low heat until cabbage is tender but still crisp, about 3 minutes.

3 Add coconut and stir well.

Cabbage and Green Peas Poriyal

[Serves 4]

 Cabbage and green peas are commonly combined in Indian cooking. Here they blend with spices in an inviting vegetable side dish.

2 tablespoons oil

1 whole dried red chili pepper

½ teaspoon mustard seeds

½ teaspoon urad dal

2 to 4 curry leaves optional

3 cups coarsely shredded cabbage

1 cup frozen green peas thawed

½ teaspoon salt more, if desired

½ teaspoon chutney powder

½ cup ground fresh coconut or unsweetened shredded coconut

1 In a skillet, heat oil over medium heat until hot, but not smoking. Add red chili pepper, mustard seeds, urad dal, and curry leaves. Fry, covered, until mustard seeds pop and urad dal is golden brown, about 30 seconds.

2 Add cabbage and stir well into seasonings. Continue cooking, uncovered, over medium heat for 1 to 2 minutes, stirring frequently.

3 Add green peas, salt, and chutney powder and stir well. Cook, covered, over medium heat for 2 minutes until cabbage and peas are cooked (do not overcook vegetables). Stir in coconut.

Carrots with Coconut Poriyal

[Serves 4]

 A delightful stir-fry of baby carrots with coconut, this poriyal can be served as a side dish with any meal.

2 cups fresh baby carrots sliced or whole

1 tablespoon oil

4 to 6 curry leaves

1 whole dried red chili pepper

½ teaspoon black mustard seeds

½ teaspoon urad dal

½ teaspoon chutney powder

½ teaspoon salt

1 teaspoon unsweetened shredded coconut

1 Steam or microwave baby carrots in a small amount of water for about 5 minutes.

2 Place oil in a skillet over medium heat. When oil is hot, but not smoking, add curry leaves, red chili pepper, mustard seeds, and urad dal. Cover and fry until mustard seeds pop and urad dal turns golden brown, about 30 seconds.

3 Add carrots to the skillet and stir well with the seasonings. Add chutney powder and salt and stir well. Cook, covered, over medium-low heat until carrots are cooked according to your taste.

4 Mix coconut with carrots and serve.

Cauliflower Kootu

[Serves 4]

 Delightfully seasoned cauliflower cooked with ginger in lentil sauce makes a great nutritious side dish!

¾ **cup moong dal (split yellow mung beans)**

½ **teaspoon ground turmeric** divided

2 **tablespoons oil**

1 **whole dried red chili pepper**

2 **to 4 curry leaves**

½ **teaspoon black mustard seeds**

½ **teaspoon urad dal**

¼ **cup chopped onions**

1 **tablespoon minced fresh ginger**

1 **teaspoon finely chopped fresh green chili pepper**

2 **cups cauliflower pieces** cut into small florets

½ **teaspoon ground cumin**

½ **teaspoon salt**

1 **tablespoon chopped cilantro**

1 Bring 4 cups of water to a boil in a saucepan. Add moong dal and ¼ teaspoon turmeric. Reduce heat to medium and cook, uncovered, for about 30 minutes, until dal is tender and creamy (if water evaporates during the cooking process, add another cup). Set aside.

2 Heat oil in a saucepan over medium heat. When oil is hot, but not smoking, add red chili pepper, curry leaves, mustard seeds, and urad dal. Cover and cook until mustard seeds pop and urad dal turns golden brown, about 30 seconds.

3 Add onions, ginger, green chili pepper, and remaining ¼ teaspoon turmeric. Stir well.

4 Add cauliflower and coat well with the seasonings.

5 Add reserved cooked dal, cumin, salt, and about ½ cup warm water. Stir cauliflower well with the dal mixture for a minute or two. Cover and cook over low heat until cauliflower is just tender, 2 to 4 minutes.

6 Add cilantro and gently mix with cauliflower.

Cauliflower Masala

[Serves 4]

 This cauliflower stir-fry with onions, tomatoes, and spices makes a colorful and tasty side dish.

3 cups cauliflower pieces cut in 1-inch to 1½-inch chunks including short stems

2 tablespoons oil

½ teaspoon black mustard seeds

½ teaspoon urad dal

½ cup chopped onions

½ cup chopped tomatoes

2 or 3 garlic cloves chopped

¼ teaspoon ground turmeric

½ teaspoon cayenne pepper powder more, if desired

½ teaspoon ground cumin

½ cup tomato sauce

1 teaspoon salt

1 Steam the cauliflower pieces until crisp-tender. Set aside.

2 Heat oil in a skillet over medium heat. When oil is hot, but not smoking, add mustard seeds and urad dal. Cover and cook until mustard seeds pop and urad dal is golden brown, about 30 seconds.

3 Add onions, tomatoes, and garlic. Stir-fry for 1 minute over medium heat.

4 Add turmeric, cayenne, and cumin. Stir well over medium heat for 1 minute. Add tomato sauce and salt. Mix well to obtain a thick paste-like consistency.

5 Add steamed cauliflower pieces and stir carefully to coat with sauce. Cook uncovered over medium heat for about 2 minutes. Be careful not to overcook!

Cauliflower, Potatoes and Green Peas

[Serves 4]

 Here is a version of alu gobi, an Indian restaurant favorite, with a few South Indian flavor twists. Enjoy it with rice or bread, or as a vegetable side dish.

1 cup cauliflower florets

2 tablespoons oil

2 to 4 curry leaves optional

½ teaspoon mustard seeds

½ teaspoon urad dal

½ cup chopped onions

1 cup chopped tomatoes

2 garlic cloves chopped

1 cup peeled and cubed potatoes

¼ teaspoon ground turmeric

½ teaspoon cayenne pepper powder

½ teaspoon ground cumin

½ teaspoon salt

½ cup frozen green peas thawed

1 Steam the cauliflower florets until crisp-tender. Set aside.

2 Put oil in skillet over medium heat. When oil is hot, but not smoking, add curry leaves, mustard seeds, and urad dal. Cover and fry until mustard seeds pop and urad dal turns golden brown, about 30 seconds.

3 Add onions, tomatoes, and garlic and sauté for a few minutes.

4 Add potatoes and stir well. Add turmeric, cayenne, cumin, and salt and stir the seasonings with the potatoes. Add 2 tablespoons of water and cover and cook over low-medium heat until potatoes are partially cooked.

5 Stir in steamed cauliflower. Cook, uncovered, for about 1 minute.

6 Stir in thawed green peas and cook briefly.

Eggplant Masala

[Serves 4]

 What could be more delicious than seasoned eggplant cooked with tomatoes and spices? This makes a tasty vegetable side and can also be served as an appetizer over crackers and flatbread.

6 baby eggplants or ½ large eggplant

5 tablespoons oil

½ teaspoon black mustard seeds

½ teaspoon urad dal

½ cup sliced onions cut lengthwise

1 cup chopped tomatoes

2 to 4 garlic cloves chopped

½ teaspoon ground turmeric

½ teaspoon cayenne pepper powder more, if desired

½ teaspoon ground cumin

1 teaspoon salt

½ cup tomato sauce

1 to 2 tablespoons unsweetened shredded coconut

1 Cut unpeeled baby eggplants into quarters or cut the large eggplant into small lengthwise pieces to make about 3 cups.

2 Place oil in a heavy skillet over medium heat. When oil is hot but not smoking, add mustard seeds and urad dal. Cover and fry until seeds are golden brown, about 30 seconds.

3 Add onion, tomatoes, and garlic. Stir-fry for a few minutes.

4 Add eggplant and turmeric and mix well. Cover and cook over medium heat, stirring often, for 2 to 3 minutes, until eggplant is slightly cooked.

5 Add cayenne, cumin, and salt. Stir in tomato sauce and mix well. Cover and cook over low heat until eggplant is tender.

6 Garnish with shredded coconut.

Eggplant and Potato Masala

[Serves 4]

 Eggplant and potato cooked in a seasoned sauce makes a delicious side dish or filling for a pita or sandwich!

6 baby eggplants or ½ large eggplant

1 cup peeled and cubed potatoes cut lengthwise 1½ x ½ inches

3 tablespoons oil

1 teaspoon cumin seeds

½ cup sliced onions cut lengthwise

1 cup chopped tomatoes

½ teaspoon ground turmeric

½ teaspoon cayenne pepper powder

½ teaspoon ground cumin

½ teaspoon salt

¼ teaspoon garam masala

1 cup tomato sauce

1 tablespoon unsweetened shredded coconut

1 Cut unpeeled eggplant(s) into pieces the same size as potatoes to make about 2 cups.

2 Place oil in a heavy skillet over medium heat. When oil is hot but not smoking, add cumin seeds. Cover and cook until seeds are golden brown.

3 Add onions and tomatoes and stir-fry for a few minutes.

4 Add potatoes and turmeric. Mix well, cover, and cook over medium heat, stirring often, for 3 to 5 minutes, until potatoes are slightly cooked.

5 Add eggplant and mix well. Add cayenne, ground cumin, salt, garam masala, and tomato sauce and mix well. (You may add about 2 tablespoons of water at this point to facilitate the cooking process.) Cover and cook over medium-low heat until vegetables are tender.

6 Add coconut and gently stir.

Eggplant Curry with Green Peas

[Serves 4]

 Aromatic, hearty eggplant curry can be served as a side dish with Adais (page 61) or breads or over rice.

1 large eggplant

1 tablespoon oil

½ teaspoon cumin seeds

1 cup finely chopped onions

½ cup finely chopped tomatoes

1 tablespoon finely minced garlic cloves

1 tablespoon grated fresh ginger

3 tablespoons tomato sauce

½ teaspoon ground turmeric

½ teaspoon ground coriander

½ teaspoon ground cumin

¼ teaspoon garam masala

¼ teaspoon cayenne pepper powder more or less to taste

¼ teaspoon salt more or less to taste

¼ cup frozen peas thawed

2 tablespoons minced fresh cilantro

1 Rub oil on eggplant and prick in several places with fork. Place on a baking sheet and bake at 400°F for 30 to 40 minutes. Let cool. Peel and discard skin, mash the pulp, and reserve 1½ cups.*

2 Heat oil in a skillet over medium-high heat. When the oil is hot but not smoking, add cumin seeds and stir until seeds change color from light brown to semi-dark brown, about 15 seconds.

3 Add onions, tomatoes, garlic, and ginger. Stir and cook for 1 to 2 minutes.

4 Add tomato sauce, turmeric, coriander, ground cumin, garam masala, cayenne, and salt. Cook for 2 to 3 minutes while stirring.

5 Add peas and the 1½ cups mashed eggplant and stir. Cook covered for 3 to 5 minutes.

6 Garnish with cilantro. Serve warm.

*Alternate preparation of eggplant in Step 1: You can also prepare the eggplant by steaming instead of baking; peel and cut eggplant in cubes and place in a pot fitted with a collapsible vegetable steamer and steam until fork tender. Then mash.

Green Beans Kootu

[Serves 4]

 This is one of my favorite ways to prepare green beans—with red lentils in a thick, creamy sauce. The seasoned butter added at the end gives the dish an extra richness.

½ cup masoor dal (red lentils)

¼ teaspoon ground turmeric

2 cups chopped green beans about ½-inch pieces

½ teaspoon ground cumin

½ teaspoon salt

1 tablespoon minced fresh ginger

1 teaspoon sambhar powder

1 tablespoon unsweetened shredded coconut

Seasoned butter

2 tablespoons unsalted butter

1 or 2 curry leaves

½ teaspoon black mustard seeds

½ teaspoon urad dal

1 Bring 2 cups of water to a boil in a saucepan. Add the masoor dal and turmeric, reduce heat to medium and cook dal, uncovered, until it becomes tender, about 20 minutes (if most of the water evaporates before dal becomes soft add an additional cup).

2 Stir in chopped green beans and cook for 3 minutes.

3 Add an additional 1 cup of water. Stir in cumin, salt, ginger, and sambhar powder. Cook until beans become tender, about 2 to 3 minutes.

4 Add coconut and stir. If the sauce is too thick add an additional ¼ cup of water and stir.

5 Melt the butter in a butter warmer or small saucepan over low heat. Add curry leaves, mustard seeds, and urad dal. After mustard seeds pop and urad dal turns golden, pour this seasoning into the cooked beans. Stir and serve warm.

VARIATIONS
For preparing **Eggplant Kootu** or **Zucchini Kootu** follow the above recipe using **2 cups cubed unpeeled eggplant or zucchini** in place of the green beans.

Green Beans with Coconut

[Serves 4]

 This recipe is quick, simple, and full of flavor. Try it instead of serving plain steamed green beans!

2 teaspoons oil

1 whole dried red chili pepper

½ teaspoon black mustard seeds

½ teaspoon urad dal

3 cups chopped green beans about ½-inch pieces

½ teaspoon chutney powder

1 teaspoon minced fresh ginger

½ teaspoon salt more, if desired

1 tablespoon unsweetened shredded coconut

1 Heat oil in a skillet over medium heat. When oil is hot, but not smoking, add red chili pepper, mustard seeds, and urad dal. Cover and fry briefly until mustard seeds pop and urad dal turns golden brown, about 30 seconds.

2 Add green beans to skillet and mix with the seasonings. Add chutney powder, ginger, and salt. Cover and cook over low-medium heat until green beans are tender.

3 Stir in coconut. Serve warm.

Green Beans with Carrots

[Serves 4 to 6]

 This vibrant, colorful stir-fry is a perfect way to enjoy two favorite vegetables that will please any palate.

2 tablespoons oil

1 whole dried red chili pepper more or less to taste

1 teaspoon black mustard seeds

1 teaspoon urad dal

2 cups chopped green beans about ½-inch pieces

2 cups peeled and chopped carrots about ½-inch pieces

1 teaspoon grated fresh ginger

½ teaspoon chutney powder

¼ teaspoon salt more or less to taste

2 tablespoons grated fresh coconut or unsweetened dried coconut

1 Heat oil in a skillet over medium-high heat. When the oil is hot but not smoking, add red chili pepper, mustard seeds, and urad dal. Stir until mustard seeds pop and urad dal turns golden, about 30 seconds.

2 Add green beans and carrots and stir-fry for about 1 minute.

3 Stir in ginger, chutney powder, and salt. Add 1 tablespoon water, cover, and cook on medium to low heat until vegetables are tender but still crisp, about 2 to 3 minutes.

4 Add coconut, stir and serve.

Green Bean Poriyal

[Serves 4]

 This fiber-rich, colorful side dish features green beans with yellow lentils, ginger, and coconut. Where I live in Milwaukee, it's also known as "Green Bay Packers Poriyal" because of its green and gold colors!

¼ **cup moong dal (split yellow mung beans)**

¼ **teaspoon ground turmeric**

2 **tablespoons oil**

2 **or 3 curry leaves** optional

½ **teaspoon black mustard seeds**

1 **teaspoon urad dal**

1 **pound green beans** stems removed and diced about ½ inch long (about 3 cups)

1 **teaspoon minced fresh ginger**

½ **fresh green chili pepper** finely chopped (optional)

½ **teaspoon salt** more, if desired

½ **teaspoon chutney powder**

1 **tablespoon unsweetened shredded coconut**

1 Bring 2 cups of water to a boil in a saucepan. Add moong dal and turmeric. Cook over medium heat, uncovered, for about 20 minutes. Drain and set aside.

2 Heat oil in a large skillet over medium heat. When oil is hot, but not smoking, stir in curry leaves, mustard seeds, and urad dal. Cover and heat until mustard seeds pop and urad dal is golden brown, about 30 seconds.

3 Add green beans, ginger, and green chili pepper and stir well. Cook over medium heat for about 1 minute.

4 Add salt and chutney powder and mix well. Cover beans and cook over low heat without water for 5 to 7 minutes. (*Note:* a sprinkle or two of water may, however, be added on top of the green beans to facilitate the cooking process.)

5 When beans are tender but still crisp, add cooked moong dal and shredded coconut. Stir well. Serve immediately or remove from heat and keep covered until serving time. Be careful not to overcook beans.

VARIATION
To make **Green Bean and Cabbage Poriyal**, use just 1½ cups diced green beans and follow the above recipe through Step 4. In Step 5, when beans are tender but still crisp, add **1½ cups coarsely shredded cabbage**. Stir-fry for about 3 minutes until cabbage is slightly cooked, then add cooked dal and shredded coconut. Stir well.

Lentil Crumble with Coconut

[Serves 4]

 This delicious, textured side dish made from split peas is rich in heart-healthy soluble fiber.

½ **cup yellow split peas**

2 **whole dried red chili peppers**

1½ **teaspoons cumin seeds** divided

1 **teaspoon fennel seeds**

3 **tablespoons oil**

1 **teaspoon black mustard seeds**

1 **cup chopped onions**

½ **teaspoon ground turmeric**

¼ **teaspoon cayenne pepper powder** more or less to taste

½ **teaspoon salt** more or less to taste

2 **tablespoons chopped cilantro**

2 **tablespoons grated fresh coconut** or unsweetened dried coconut

1 Place split peas in a bowl and cover with hot water. Let soak for 30 minutes.

2 Drain the split peas and put in a blender or food processor with red chili peppers, 1 teaspoon cumin seeds, fennel seeds, and ¼ cup of warm water. Blend or process until the texture of coarse cornmeal. Pour mixture into a microwave-safe dish, cover with a small plate, and cook on high for 3 minutes—mixture will feel somewhat firm. Cool for 5 minutes and then break into small pieces with a fork. Reserve the crumble.

3 Heat oil in a skillet over medium-high heat. When the oil is hot but not smoking, add black mustard seeds and remaining ½ teaspoon cumin seeds and stir until mustard seeds start to pop and cumin seeds change color from light brown to semi-dark brown.

4 Add onions and cook for 30 seconds while stirring.

5 Add reserved split pea crumble mixture, turmeric, cayenne, and salt. Continue to cook over medium-low heat for 2 to 4 minutes, while stirring, until the split pea crumble becomes golden and grainy in texture.

6 Add cilantro and coconut, stir and serve.

Heavenly Lima Bean Masala

[Serves 4 to 6]

 This recipe has become a favorite among my television program viewers. Lima beans are simmered with seasonings in tomato sauce to make a heavenly side dish. It can also be enjoyed as a sandwich filling with pita bread.

1 package (16 ounces) frozen baby lima
    beans thawed (about 2½ cups)

3 tablespoons oil

2 or 3 (½-inch-long) slivers cinnamon stick

½ teaspoon black mustard seeds

½ teaspoon urad dal

½ cup chopped onions

½ cup chopped tomatoes

½ teaspoon ground turmeric

½ teaspoon cayenne pepper powder more
    if desired

½ teaspoon ground cumin

1 teaspoon salt

1 cup tomato sauce

2 tablespoons unsweetened shredded dried
    coconut

1 Bring ¾ cup of water to a boil in a saucepan. Add lima beans and return to boil. Reduce heat to medium, cover, and cook on low heat for 5 to 7 minutes, stirring occasionally. Set aside.

2 Place oil in a skillet over medium heat. When oil is hot, but not smoking, add slivers of cinnamon stick, mustard seeds, and urad dal. Cover and cook over medium heat until mustard seeds pop and urad dal is golden brown, about 30 seconds.

3 Add onions and tomatoes and stir for a few minutes. Add turmeric and stir well over medium heat. Add cayenne, cumin, and salt and stir well for 1 minute. Add tomato sauce.

4 When mixture begins to boil, add undrained cooked lima beans and stir well. Cover and cook over medium heat until lima beans are tender.

5 Add coconut and stir well.

Lima Beans Poriyal with Coconut

[Serves 4]

 Even if you dislike lima beans, you will be in for a pleasant surprise when you try this dish. Lima beans are packed with protein and fiber and this is an easy-to-prepare lima bean stir-fry with coconut. A great side dish and a healthy snack!

1 package (10 to 16 ounces) frozen baby or Fordhook (large) lima beans

2 tablespoons oil

2 to 4 curry leaves optional

1 whole dried red chili pepper

½ teaspoon black mustard seeds

½ teaspoon urad dal

1 teaspoon chutney powder

1 teaspoon salt

1 tablespoon unsweetened shredded coconut

1 Cook lima beans in microwave or on stovetop according to package direction. Drain and set side.

2 Place oil in a skillet over medium heat. When oil is hot, but not smoking, stir in curry leaves, red chili pepper, mustard seeds, and urad dal. Cover and fry until mustard seeds pop and urad dal is golden brown, about 30 seconds.

3 Add drained lima beans and stir-fry for a few minutes over medium heat.

4 Add chutney powder and salt and stir to coat the lima beans with the seasonings. Add shredded coconut, stir, and serve warm.

Mushroom Masala

[Serves 4]

 Lightly seasoned mushrooms cooked in tomato sauce make a delicious side dish.

1 teaspoon oil

½ teaspoon cumin seeds

½ cup chopped onions

¼ cup chopped tomatoes

1 tablespoon tomato sauce

¼ teaspoon cayenne pepper powder

½ teaspoon ground cumin

½ teaspoon salt

2 cups (8 ounces) white button mushrooms
  cut in half

1 Place oil in a skillet over medium heat. When oil is hot, but not smoking, add cumin seeds and cook for about 30 seconds. Immediately add the onions and tomatoes and stir-fry for a few minutes.

2 Add tomato sauce, cayenne, ground cumin, and salt. When the mixture thickens, add mushrooms and stir well. Cook mushrooms, uncovered, on low heat for 3 minutes.

Mushrooms with Onion and Garlic

[Serves 4]

 This easy-to-prepare mushroom dish, seasoned with ginger, cumin, and garlic, makes a tasty accompaniment to any main dish.

8 ounces fresh mushrooms white button, shiitake, cremini, and/or portabella

1 tablespoon oil

½ teaspoon cumin seeds

½ medium onion sliced lengthwise

1½ teaspoons grated fresh ginger

4 garlic cloves minced

½ teaspoon Black Pepper and Cumin Powder (page 4)

¼ teaspoon salt more or less to taste

2 tablespoons chopped red onion

1 Rinse and dry mushrooms thoroughly and then slice.

2 Heat oil in a skillet over medium-high heat until hot but not smoking. Add cumin seeds and stir until seeds change color from light brown to semi-dark brown.

3 Add onion, ginger, and garlic. Cook for 1 minute while stirring. Add sliced mushrooms, Black Pepper and Cumin Powder, and salt. Stir-fry for 3 to 5 minutes over medium-high heat.

4 Add red onion and serve.

Okra Masala

[Serves 4]

 Lightly seasoned and simmered with tomatoes and spices, this okra is a favorite in Indian cuisine. Okra Masala (also known as Bhindi Masala) goes well with any flavored or plain rice dish.

2 tablespoons oil

¼ teaspoon asafoetida powder

½ teaspoon black mustard seeds

½ teaspoon urad dal

½ cup chopped onions

½ cup chopped tomatoes

½ teaspoon ground turmeric

½ teaspoon cayenne pepper powder

½ teaspoon ground cumin

½ cup tomato sauce

1 teaspoon salt

3 cups sliced fresh or frozen and thawed okra

1 tablespoon unsweetened shredded coconut

1 Place oil in skillet over medium heat. When oil is hot, but not smoking, add asafoetida powder, mustard seeds, and urad dal. Cover and fry until mustard seeds pop and urad dal turns golden brown, about 30 seconds.

2 Add onions and tomatoes and stir-fry for 1 minute. Add turmeric, cayenne, cumin, tomato sauce, and salt. Cook for 1 to 2 minutes.

3 Add okra and stir-fry for 3 to 5 minutes. Cover and cook over low heat until okra is tender.

4 Add coconut and gently stir for an additional minute.

Potatoes and Tomatoes in Lentil Sauce

[Serves 4]

 The delicate flavors of the spices and tomatoes bring this potato lentil dish to life. It's like having dal but with the extra heartiness of potatoes added. Serve over plain rice or quinoa, or with naan bread.

½ cup moong dal (split yellow mung beans)

¾ teaspoon ground turmeric divided

1 cup scrubbed and cubed potatoes (about 1½-inch cubes)

3 tablespoons oil

1 whole dried red chili pepper

1 teaspoon cumin seeds

½ cup chopped onions

1 cup chopped tomatoes

1 teaspoon ground cumin

½ teaspoon cayenne pepper powder more or less to taste

¼ teaspoon salt more or less to taste

½ cup chopped fresh cilantro

1 Bring 3 cups of water to a boil in a 1-quart saucepan. Add moong dal and ¼ teaspoon turmeric. Reduce heat to medium and cook, uncovered, for about 30 minutes, until dal softens (if water evaporates during the cooking process, add another ½ cup). Do not drain. Mash moong dal with potato masher. Reserve.

2 Parboil the potatoes until partially cooked. Drain and set aside.

3 Heat oil in a skillet over medium-high heat. When the oil is hot but not smoking, add red chili pepper and cumin seeds. Stir until cumin seeds change color from light brown to semi-dark brown, about 30 seconds.

4 Add onions, tomatoes, ground cumin, cayenne, and remaining ½ teaspoon turmeric. Cook about 2 to 3 minutes or until onions are tender.

5 Add reserved mashed moong dal, parboiled potatoes, salt, and cilantro; stir to combine. Bring to a simmer. Reduce heat to low and simmer about 3 to 5 minutes until potatoes are tender, stirring occasionally and adding up to ½ cup of warm water, if needed.

Potato Kurma

[Serves 4]

 Potatoes cooked in a delectable coconut and almond-based sauce, Potato Kurma can be served over plain rice, with a rice pilaf, with naan or plain toasted bread, or with warm whole wheat tortillas.

½ cup unsweetened shredded coconut

2 fresh green chili peppers more, if desired

16 raw almonds

2 teaspoons cumin seeds divided

1 teaspoon fennel seeds divided

2 thick slices fresh ginger

1 tablespoon oil

1 tablespoon unsalted butter

2 to 4 curry leaves optional

1 bay leaf

2 to 4 (½-inch-long) slivers cinnamon sticks

1 cup coarsely chopped onions

2 cups chopped tomatoes divided

2 cups peeled and cubed Idaho potatoes
 (about 1-inch cubes)

½ teaspoon ground turmeric

1 teaspoon curry powder

1 teaspoon salt more, if desired

¼ cup chopped fresh cilantro leaves

1 In a blender put coconut, green chili peppers, almonds, 1 teaspoon cumin seeds, ½ teaspoon fennel seeds, ginger, and 2 cups hot water. Grind into a smooth paste.

2 Place oil and butter in a wide-bottomed saucepan over medium heat. When oil is hot but not smoking, add curry leaves, bay leaf, cinnamon sticks, remaining 1 teaspoon cumin seeds, and remaining ½ teaspoon fennel seeds. Stir-fry to a golden brown.

3 Add onions and 1 cup chopped tomatoes and stir-fry for a few minutes.

4 Add potatoes and turmeric and stir well for 1 minute. Add curry powder and stir the seasonings well with potatoes for couple of minutes.

5 Add the coconut spice paste from the blender along with salt and 2 cups of warm water and mix thoroughly.

6 When mixture begins to boil, add the remaining 1 cup of chopped tomatoes and cook covered over medium-low heat until potatoes are tender.

7 Add cilantro and serve.

VARIATION
To prepare **Potato and Pea Kurma**, add **1 cup thawed frozen green peas** to the above sauce in Step 6. A colorful delicious blend of potatoes and peas in kurma sauce!

Potato Masala

[Serves 4 to 6]

 These seasoned potatoes with tomatoes and ginger are a wonderful alternative to plain mashed potatoes. This recipe can be used as a filling for samosas, masala dosais (page 67), or sandwiches. It also works well on its own as a delicious side dish!

2 medium Idaho potatoes with skins cut in quarters

½ teaspoon ground turmeric divided

1 teaspoon salt divided

2 tablespoons oil

¼ teaspoon asafoetida powder

2 to 4 curry leaves optional

½ teaspoon black mustard seeds

½ teaspoon urad dal

1 cup chopped onions

½ cup chopped tomatoes

1 fresh green chili pepper chopped

1 tablespoon minced fresh ginger

½ teaspoon cayenne pepper powder

¼ cup minced fresh cilantro leaves

1 Cook potatoes with sufficient water to cover with ¼ teaspoon turmeric and ½ teaspoon salt in a covered saucepan over medium heat for approximately 20 minutes or until potatoes become soft. Drain, peel, and coarsely chop potatoes; set aside.

2 In a skillet, heat oil over medium heat. When oil is hot, but not smoking, add asafoetida powder, curry leaves, mustard seeds, and urad dal. Cover and cook until mustard seeds pop and urad dal is golden brown, about 30 seconds.

3 Add onions, tomatoes, green chili pepper, and ginger. Stir-fry for 1 minute. Add the remaining ¼ teaspoon turmeric, remaining ½ teaspoon salt, and the cayenne. Stir well.

4 Add coarsely chopped potatoes and stir gently with ingredients in skillet. Cover and cook over medium heat for 2 to 3 minutes, so flavors will blend well. Taste for seasonings and add more salt, if desired. Add cilantro and mix well.

Roasted Potato Medley

[Serves 4 to 6]

 In this dish, yukon gold and sweet potatoes are seasoned with garlic and simple spices. This colorful dish is an excellent accompaniment to any main course.

¾ **pound Yukon Gold potatoes** peeled and cut into cubes (1½ cups)

¾ **pound sweet potatoes** peeled and cut into cubes (1½ cups)

½ **teaspoon ground turmeric**

⅛ **teaspoon salt** more or less to taste

¼ **teaspoon cayenne pepper powder** more or less to taste

2 **tablespoons oil**

2 **garlic cloves** chopped

¼ **cup chopped green onions**

1 Place cubed potatoes and sweet potatoes in a large glass bowl with ¼ cup of water and cook in microwave on high for 2 minutes; or place in saucepan and boil/steam for 5 minutes on stovetop. They should just be partially cooked and still firm. Drain.

2 Mix together turmeric, salt, and cayenne. Sprinkle on potato mixture and toss until spices are evenly coating them.

3 Heat oil in a skillet over medium-high heat. When the oil is hot but not smoking, add the seasoned potato pieces and garlic to skillet. Cook over medium-low heat for 3 to 5 minutes, stirring to prevent sticking, until potatoes become golden and crisp. (Alternatively, you can spread them on a dark baking sheet and bake at 425°F until crisp.)

4 Sprinkle with green onions, stir and serve.

Seasoned Roasted Potatoes with Garlic

[Serves 4]

 Lightly seasoned and pan-fried, these potatoes are particularly delicious served with any flavored rice or meat dish.

2 cups peeled and cubed Idaho potatoes
(1-inch cubes)

¼ teaspoon ground turmeric

½ teaspoon salt

½ teaspoon cayenne pepper powder more,
if desired

½ teaspoon ground cumin

2 tablespoons oil

2 tablespoons chopped garlic cloves

1 Place the cubed potatoes in a glass bowl with ¼ cup water and cook in microwave on high for 2 minutes; or steam potatoes for 3 to 5 minutes on stovetop. Potatoes should still be firm. Drain.

2 Mix together turmeric, salt, cayenne, and cumin. Sprinkle on potatoes and toss until potatoes are evenly coated with spices.

3 Heat oil in a skillet over medium-high heat. When the oil is hot but not smoking, add the seasoned potato pieces and garlic to skillet. Cook over medium-low heat for 3 to 5 minutes, stirring to prevent sticking, until potatoes become golden and crisp. (*Alternatively,* you can spread the potatoes and garlic on a dark baking sheet and bake at 425ºF until crisp.)

Seasoned Tri-Colored Bell Peppers

[Serves 4]

 Crunchy, delicious bell peppers are also rich in Vitamin C. This vibrant, colorful side dish is a perfect way to celebrate summer's bounty of bell peppers.

1 each red, yellow, and green bell peppers

2 teaspoons oil

1 teaspoon black mustard seeds

¼ teaspoon cumin seeds

¼ cup chopped onions

¼ teaspoon cayenne pepper powder

¼ teaspoon ground cumin

½ teaspoon salt

1 teaspoon unsweetened shredded coconut

1 Dice bell peppers into 1-inch cubes (about 2 cups mixed); set aside.

2 Heat oil in a skillet over medium heat. When the oil is hot but not smoking, add the mustard seeds and cumin seeds. Stir until mustard seeds pop and cumin seeds turns slightly brown, about 30 seconds.

3 Add onions and stir-fry for 30 seconds. Add the bell peppers, cayenne, ground cumin, and salt. Stir-fry for 3 minutes or until peppers are crisp-tender.

4 Add coconut, stir, and serve.

Spinach Kootu

[Serves 4 to 6]

 This mild and delicate spinach in lentil sauce can be served over quinoa or rice or as a side dish.

1 cup masoor dal (red lentils) or **moong dal (split yellow mung beans)**

¼ **teaspoon ground turmeric**

2 **tablespoons oil**

1 **whole dried red chili pepper**

½ **teaspoon black mustard seeds**

½ **teaspoon urad dal**

¼ **cup chopped onions**

4 **garlic cloves** minced

1 **package (10 ounces) frozen chopped spinach** thawed*

1 **teaspoon ground cumin**

1 **teaspoon salt**

1 **fresh green chili pepper** chopped (optional)

*You may also use chopped fresh baby spinach instead of the frozen spinach. Fresh spinach when cooked becomes wilted and results in a smaller quantity but fresh spinach enhances the flavor.

1 Bring 4 cups of water to a boil. Add dal and turmeric. Reduce heat to medium-high and cook, uncovered, for about 20 to 30 minutes until dal becomes creamy (if water evaporates during the cooking process, add another cup). Set aside.

2 Heat oil in a saucepan over medium heat. When oil is hot, but not smoking, stir in red chili pepper, mustard seeds, and urad dal. Cover and fry until mustard seeds pop and urad dal is golden brown, about 30 seconds.

3 Add onions and garlic and stir-fry for approximately 1 minute.

4 Stir in thawed spinach, cooked dal, and 1 cup of warm water and stir. Add cumin, salt, and green chili pepper, if desired. Stir well with ingredients in saucepan.

5 Cover and cook over low heat for another 5 to 7 minutes, until spinach is cooked and all flavors are thoroughly blended.

Spinach Poriyal with Lentils and Coconut

[Serves 4]

 This colorful, wholesome spinach blend can be served as a side dish or used to make Spinach Rice with Cashews (page 96) or Stuffed Baby Portabella Mushrooms (page 33).

½ **cup masoor dal (red lentils)** or **moong dal (split yellow mung beans)**

¼ **teaspoon ground turmeric**

1 **tablespoon oil**

½ **teaspoon mustard seeds**

½ **teaspoon urad dal**

1 **cup chopped onions**

1 **fresh green chili pepper** chopped (more or less to taste)

1 **(10 to 16-ounce) package frozen chopped spinach** thawed

½ **teaspoon salt** more or less to taste

2 **tablespoons grated fresh coconut** or **unsweetened shredded coconut**

1 Bring 2 cups of water to a boil in a saucepan. Add dal and turmeric and cook uncovered until soft, about 15 minutes (if water evaporates before dal becomes tender, add an additional ¼ cup). Do not drain; reserve.

2 Heat oil in a skillet over medium heat. When the oil is hot but not smoking, add mustard seeds and urad dal. Stir until mustard seeds pop and urad dal turns golden, about 30 seconds.

3 Add onions and green chili pepper and stir-fry for 1 minute.

4 Add thawed spinach, 1 tablespoon of water, and salt. Stir well, cover, and cook over medium heat about 4 minutes or until spinach is tender, stirring occasionally.

5 Add reserved cooked dal to spinach mixture. Stir thoroughly and cook for 1 minute over medium heat. Add coconut, stir, and serve.

VARIATION
You may add ½ **teaspoon ground cumin** or ½ **teaspoon chutney powder** in Step 4 to add more depth of flavor.

Summer Squash Medley

[Serves 4]

 Zucchini and yellow squash combined with chili peppers and spices make a tasty and colorful side dish.

1 tablespoon oil

1 whole dried red chili pepper

½ teaspoon black mustard seeds

½ teaspoon cumin seeds

1½ cups cubed zucchini

1½ cups cubed yellow squash

¼ teaspoon ground turmeric

½ **fresh green chili pepper** minced (more or less to taste)

¼ **teaspoon salt** more or less to taste

2 tablespoons grated fresh coconut or unsweetened dried coconut

1 Heat oil in a skillet over medium-high heat. When the oil is hot but not smoking, add the red chili pepper, mustard seeds, and cumin seeds and stir until mustard seeds start to pop and cumin seeds change color from light brown to semi-dark brown, about 30 seconds.

2 Add zucchini, yellow squash, turmeric, green chili pepper, and salt. Stir-fry over medium-low heat for 2 minutes.

3 Stir in coconut and serve.

Sweet Potato Poriyal I

[Makes 2 cups]

 These are simple, lightly seasoned recipes that enhance the natural, hearty flavor of sweet potatoes. Perfect for weeknight dinners! The second version is cooked on the stovetop instead of roasting in oven.

1 pound sweet potatoes peeled and cut into 1-inch cubes (about 2 cups)

½ teaspoon cayenne pepper powder more or less to taste

½ teaspoon ground cumin

⅛ teaspoon salt more or less to taste

½ tablespoon grated fresh coconut or **unsweetened dried coconut**

1 Preheat oven to 400°F. Steam sweet potatoes in a saucepan about 5 minutes or until tender.

2 Combine cayenne, cumin, salt, and coconut in a small dish. Sprinkle over cooked sweet potatoes and toss gently to coat.

3 Place seasoned sweet potatoes on a dark, shallow baking sheet and spray with cooking spray. Bake in oven until starting to brown.

Sweet Potato Poriyal II

1 pound sweet potatoes peeled and cut into 1-inch cubes (about 2 cups)

1 tablespoon oil

1 whole dried red chili pepper

½ teaspoon black mustard seeds

¼ teaspoon cumin seeds

½ teaspoon chutney powder

¼ teaspoon salt

1 tablespoon unsweetened shredded coconut

1 Steam sweet potatoes in a saucepan about 5 minutes until tender. Set aside.

2 Heat oil in a skillet over medium heat. When the oil is hot but not smoking, add the red chili pepper, mustard seeds, and cumin seeds. Stir until mustard seeds start to pop and cumin seeds change color to light brown, about 30 seconds.

3 Add steamed sweet potatoes, chutney powder, and salt. Gently mix with the seasonings for a minute. Add coconut and gently mix. Serve warm.

Swiss Chard Lentil Crumble

[Serves 6]

 A unique and innovative colorful Swiss chard dish enhanced with yellow split peas and coconut.

⅓ **cup yellow split peas**

1 **whole dried red chili pepper** more or less
   to taste

½ **teaspoon fennel seeds**

1½ **teaspoons cumin seeds** divided

3 **tablespoons oil**

½ **teaspoon black mustard seeds**

1 **cup chopped onions**

½ **teaspoon ground turmeric**

½ **teaspoon cayenne pepper powder** more
   or less to taste

¼ **teaspoon salt** more or less to taste

4 **cups chopped Swiss chard including
   stems**

3 **tablespoons grated fresh coconut** or
   unsweetened dried coconut

VARIATION
You can make **Broccoli Lentil Crumble** or
Spinach Lentil Crumble by substituting
4 **cups fresh chopped broccoli** or 4 **cups
fresh baby spinach** for the swiss chard.

1 Place split peas in a bowl and add enough hot water to cover. Let soak for 30 minutes. Drain.

2 Place soaked and drained peas in a blender or food processor with red chili pepper, fennel seeds, cumin seeds, and ¼ cup of warm water. Blend or process until the texture of coarse cornmeal. Pour mixture in a microwave-safe dish, cover with paper towel, and cook on high for 3 minutes—mixture will feel somewhat firm. Cool for 5 minutes; break into small pieces with a fork; reserve crumble.

3 Heat oil in a skillet over medium-high heat. When the oil is hot but not smoking, add mustard seeds and cumin seeds and stir until mustard seeds start to pop and cumin seeds change color from light brown to semi-dark brown, about 30 seconds.

4 Add onions and stir-fry for 30 seconds.

5 Add reserved split pea crumble, turmeric, cayenne, and salt. Stir well. Continue to stir while cooking over medium-low heat for 3 to 5 minutes, until the split peas become golden and grainy in texture.

6 Stir in Swiss chard, cover, and cook over low heat 3 to 5 minutes until chard becomes tender, stirring frequently.

7 Add coconut, stir, and serve.

Vegetable Kurma

[Serves 6]

 Vegetable Kurma is a specialty in Chettinad cooking. A colorful blend of hearty vegetables is cooked in a delicately spiced coconut almond sauce. Serve with rice or bread.

2 cups peeled and cubed Idaho potato
   (1 inch)

1 tablespoon unsalted butter

1 tablespoon oil

2 to 4 curry leaves optional

1 bay leaf

3 or 4 (½-inch-long) slivers cinnamon sticks

¼ teaspoon cumin seeds

¼ teaspoon fennel seeds

1 cup chopped onions

1 cup chopped tomatoes divided

1½ cups cauliflower florets

½ teaspoon ground turmeric

1 teaspoon curry powder

½ teaspoon salt more, if desired

1 cup frozen peas and carrots thawed

Spice Paste

½ cup unsweetened shredded coconut

1 fresh green chili pepper more, if desired

14 raw almonds

1 tablespoon white poppy seeds optional

1 teaspoon cumin seeds

1 teaspoon fennel seeds

2 thick slices fresh ginger

1 Place all the ingredients for the spice paste in a blender. Add 2 cups of hot water and grind the ingredients to a smooth paste. Set aside.

2 Par-boil the cubed potatoes: in a bowl place cubed potatoes with one tablespoon water and microwave on high for 2 to 3 minutes. Set aside.

3 Heat butter and oil in a wide-bottomed saucepan over medium heat. When oil is hot but not smoking, add curry leaves, bay leaf, cinnamon sticks, cumin seeds, and fennel seeds. Cover and fry to a golden brown, about 30 seconds.

4 Add onions and ½ cup of the chopped tomatoes and stir-fry for 1 minute until onions are lightly translucent.

5 Add par-boiled potatoes, cauliflower florets, and turmeric and stir well. Add curry powder and salt and stir-fry for 1 to 2 minutes. Add spice paste from blender and 2 cups of hot water. Stir the mixture and cook for 2 to 3 minutes.

6 Add thawed carrots and peas and 1 cup of warm water and cook for 2 minutes. Add the remaining ½ cup tomatoes and gently stir. Cover and cook for a couple of minutes until the flavors are blended together.

7 Add another ½ cup warm water (or coconut cream) if needed to get desired consistency. Stir and serve.

Roasted Vegetables

[Serves 6]

 I like to make this colorful blend of roasted vegetables in autumn when most of the items are in season. With simple, light seasoning, the flavors of the vegetables really shine.

4 tablespoons oil

1 teaspoon ground cumin

½ teaspoon ground coriander

¼ teaspoon cayenne pepper powder more or less to taste

¼ teaspoon salt more or less to taste

5 cups raw vegetables cut into pieces, such as:

   1 cup broccoli florets cut in half

   1 cup cauliflower florets cut in half

   1 cup Brussels sprouts stem end cut off and cut in half

   1 cup peeled and cubed sweet potato

   1 cup peeled and cubed butternut squash

1 Preheat oven to 425°F.

2 In a large bowl, combine oil, cumin, coriander, cayenne, and salt.

3 Add vegetables and toss to coat. Spread out in a single layer on a shallow dark baking sheet. (Note: dark baking sheets work best for browning; also if vegetables are too close to each other, they will steam instead of roasting.)

4 Place in oven and roast 10 minutes. Check to see if they are starting to brown. If not, return to oven for 5 minutes. When edges are browned, stir and bake 10 minutes longer or until vegetables reach desired softness. (Cooking time will vary based on your individual oven and how well done you like your vegetables.)

Non-Vegetarian Dishes

Egg Kulambu

[Serves 4]

 A unique way to enjoy hard-boiled eggs is cooking them with spices in an aromatic tamarind sauce. This saucy dish can be served over plain rice or as an accompaniment to idlis (page 73), dosais (page 65), and naan breads.

2 tablespoons oil

2 or 3 (½-inch-long) slivers cinnamon stick

1 dried bay leaf

2 to 4 curry leaves optional

¼ teaspoon fenugreek seeds

¼ teaspoon urad dal

¼ teaspoon cumin seeds

¼ teaspoon fennel seeds

½ cup chopped onions

¼ cup chopped tomatoes

4 garlic cloves quartered

½ fresh green chili pepper chopped

¼ teaspoon ground turmeric

1 teaspoon curry powder

½ teaspoon cayenne pepper powder

¼ teaspoon tamarind paste

1 teaspoon Black Pepper and Cumin Powder
(page 4)

1 teaspoon salt

1 cup tomato sauce*

¼ cup finely chopped fresh cilantro leaves

4 large hard-boiled eggs peeled

*You can add an additional ½ cup of tomato sauce for a milder taste.

1 Heat oil in a saucepan over medium heat. When oil is hot, but not smoking, add cinnamon stick, bay leaf, curry leaves, fenugreek seeds, urad dal, cumin seeds, and fennel seeds. Stir gently and cover and cook until seeds pop and urad dal is golden brown, about 30 seconds.

2 Immediately add onions, tomatoes, garlic, and chili pepper. Stir and add turmeric. When onions are tender, add curry powder, cayenne, tamarind paste, Black Pepper and Cumin Powder, salt, tomato sauce, and 1 cup of water. Mix well and allow the mixture to come to a boil, then lower heat and simmer for about 2 minutes. Add cilantro.

3 Score the hard-boiled eggs with cross marks on each end and add the eggs to the simmering sauce and spoon the sauce over the eggs so they will absorb the flavor of the sauce.

4 Remove from heat. Cover and let the eggs soak in the sauce for 5 to 7 minutes and serve.

Egg Curry

[Serves 4]

 Hard-boiled eggs soak up delicate flavors when coated in a rich, seasoned sauce. You can serve this over rice or quinoa.

1 teaspoon oil

¼ teaspoon cumin seeds

¼ cup chopped onions

¼ cup chopped tomatoes

2 garlic cloves coarsely chopped

¼ teaspoon ground turmeric

¼ teaspoon cayenne pepper powder

¼ teaspoon ground cumin

½ teaspoon Black Pepper and Cumin Powder (page 4)

½ teaspoon salt

¼ cup tomato sauce

4 hard-boiled eggs peeled

1 Heat the oil in a small skillet or wok over medium heat. When oil is hot, but not smoking, add the cumin seeds and stir-fry for 30 seconds. Immediately add the onions, tomatoes, garlic, and turmeric and stir for 1 minute.

2 When onions are tender, add cayenne, ground cumin, Black Pepper and Cumin Powder, salt, and tomato sauce. Stir well to mix all the ingredients and cook, uncovered, over medium heat for 2 to 3 minutes. Lower the heat.

3 Score the hard-boiled eggs with cross marks on each end with tip of knife and add to the simmering sauce, spooning sauce over the eggs. Cover and remove from heat and allow eggs to stay in the sauce for 5 to 7 minutes before serving so they can absorb the flavor of the sauce.

Chettinad Chicken Masala

[Serves 4]

 Tender pieces of chicken in a ginger-garlic sauce—a Chettinad specialty! This dish is relatively simple to prepare and flavors are outstanding! Serve with rice or naan.

1 pound chicken pieces (about 4 thighs or halved breasts with or without bones)

2 tablespoons oil

2 to 4 curry leaves optional

1 bay leaf

2 slivers (½-inch-long) cinnamon stick

¼ teaspoon fennel seeds

¼ teaspoon cumin seeds

½ cup chopped onions

¼ cup chopped tomatoes

4 garlic cloves chopped

2 tablespoons minced fresh ginger

½ teaspoon ground turmeric

2 teaspoons curry powder

1 teaspoon salt

1 teaspoon Black Pepper and Cumin Powder (page 4)

½ cup tomato sauce

1 Remove skin from chicken pieces and cut into small stew-size pieces (with or without bones). Set aside.

2 Heat oil in a skillet over medium heat. When oil is hot, but not smoking, add curry leaves, bay leaf, cinnamon sticks, fennel seeds, and cumin seeds. Stir until cumin seeds become brown, about 30 seconds.

3 Add onions, tomatoes, garlic, ginger, and turmeric and stir well for 1 minute.

4 Add chicken pieces. Brown well and cook on high heat until chicken become opaque (partially cooked).

5 Reduce heat and add curry powder, salt, and Black Pepper and Cumin Powder. Stir well. Add tomato sauce and stir well.

6 Cover and cook over medium-low heat until chicken becomes tender and has absorbed the flavors of the sauce, about 20 to 30 minutes. (Note: During the cooking process, check often and stir frequently to prevent the chicken from sticking to skillet, adding 1 to 2 tablespoons of water if needed.)

Chicken Curry in a Hurry

[Serves 4]

 This simple version of chicken in seasoned sauce can be served over rice or with naan bread. It is a lighter version of chicken tikka masala, without butter and heavy cream.

3 tablespoons oil

2 or 3 (½-inch-long) slivers cinnamon sticks

1 bay leaf

½ cup chopped onions

½ cup chopped tomatoes

3 garlic cloves quartered

2 tablespoons minced fresh ginger

¼ teaspoon ground turmeric

1 pound skinless boneless chicken breasts
  or thighs cut into stew-size piece

½ teaspoon salt

2 teaspoons curry powder

1 teaspoon Black Pepper and Cumin Powder
  (page 4)

1 cup tomato sauce

2 tablespoons chopped fresh cilantro

1 Heat oil in a wide saucepan over medium heat. When oil is hot, but not smoking, add cinnamon sticks and bay leaf and cook for about 30 seconds.

2 Add onions, tomatoes, and garlic and stir-fry for 1 minute. Stir in turmeric.

3 Add chicken pieces to saucepan and brown for 2 to 4 minutes.

4 Add salt, curry powder, and Black Pepper and Cumin Powder. Stir to coat the chicken well with the spices. Add tomato sauce and stir.

5 Cover and cook, stirring often, until chicken is tender, about 20 minutes. Add cilantro. (If the sauce becomes too thick, you may add small amounts of both water and tomato sauce as desired.)

Chicken Kurma

[Serves 4]

 Tender pieces of chicken are simmered in a rich, fragrant coconut almond sauce. Serve over rice or quinoa.

2 pounds skinless chicken pieces (thighs or boneless breasts)

2 tablespoons oil

1 tablespoon unsalted butter

1 bay leaf

2 to 4 (½-inch-long) slivers cinnamon sticks

½ teaspoon cumin seeds

½ teaspoon fennel seeds

½ cup onion slices cut lengthwise

½ cup chopped tomatoes

½ teaspoon ground turmeric

2 teaspoons curry powder

½ teaspoon garam masala

1 teaspoon salt more or less to taste

¼ cup minced fresh cilantro

Spice Paste

2 small slices fresh ginger

1 fresh green chili pepper more or less to taste

1 garlic clove

1 teaspoon fennel seeds

1 tablespoon poppy seeds optional

1 teaspoon cumin seeds

16 raw almonds

½ cup unsweetened shredded dried coconut

2 cups hot water

1 Wipe chicken with a damp paper towel. Cut into 2-inch pieces. Reserve.

2 Place all spice paste ingredients in a food processor or blender. Process for about 5 minutes into a creamy smooth paste. Reserve.

3 Heat oil and butter in a skillet over medium-high heat. When the oil is hot but not smoking add bay leaf, cinnamon sticks, cumin seeds, and fennel seeds and stir until seeds change color from light brown to semi-dark brown, about 30 seconds.

4 Add onions, tomatoes, and turmeric and stir-fry for about 2 to 3 minutes.

5 Add reserved chicken and sauté over medium-high heat for 3 to 5 minutes until chicken starts to brown.

6 Stir in curry powder, garam masala, and salt. Add reserved spice paste from blender. Stir and cook over medium heat for 3 minutes. Add additional 1 cup of warm water and stir.

7 Cover and cook over medium-low heat, stirring occasionally, about 15 to 20 minutes or until chicken is tender.

8 Add cilantro and cook for 1 more minute.

Chicken with Potatoes in Ginger Garlic Sauce

[Serves 4]

 Chicken with potatoes in an aromatic sauce makes a hearty meal. Serve over rice or quinoa.

1 pound boneless skinless chicken breasts or thighs

2 tablespoons oil

1 bay leaf

¼ teaspoon cumin seeds

¼ teaspoon fennel seeds

2 (½-inch-long) slivers cinnamon stick

½ cup chopped onions

½ cup chopped tomatoes

6 whole garlic cloves

½ teaspoon ground turmeric

1 cup cubed Yukon Gold or russet potatoes

2 teaspoons curry powder

1 teaspoon Black Pepper and Cumin Powder (page 4)

1 teaspoon salt more or less to taste

2 tablespoons grated fresh ginger

1 cup tomato sauce

¼ cup chopped fresh cilantro

1 Wipe chicken with a damp paper towel. Cut into stew-size pieces; reserve.

2 Heat oil in a skillet over medium-high heat. When the oil is hot but not smoking add bay leaf, cumin seeds, fennel seeds, and cinnamon stick. Stir until cumin seeds change color from light brown to semi-dark brown, about 30 seconds.

3 Add onions, tomatoes, garlic, and turmeric. Stir-fry for 2 to 3 minutes.

4 Add chicken and brown over medium-high heat for 3 to 5 minutes.

5 Stir in potatoes, curry powder, Black Pepper and Cumin Powder, salt, ginger, tomato sauce, and 2 cups warm water. Bring to a simmer. Cover and cook over medium-low heat about 15 to 20 minutes, stirring occasionally, until chicken is tender and potatoes are cooked.

6 Add cilantro and cook 1 minute.

Spice-Rubbed Roasted Chicken

[Serves 4 or 5]

 Roasting whole spices is one of the best methods of drawing out their rich flavors. You will see what a difference it makes. In this recipe, spice-coated chicken becomes extra tender and flavorful as it slowly roasts in the oven. You can use chicken thighs or breasts, turkey breasts, or Cornish hens.

5 skinless chicken thighs (about 1½ pounds)

¼ cup yellow split peas

1 tablespoon black peppercorns

1 tablespoon cumin seeds

2 whole dried red chili peppers more or less to taste

2 teaspoons coriander seeds

½ teaspoon salt more or less to taste

½ teaspoon ground turmeric

2 teaspoons finely minced garlic cloves

¼ cup oil

1 Wipe chicken with a damp paper towel.

2 To dry roast spices, place yellow split peas, peppercorns, cumin seeds, red chili peppers, and coriander seeds in a small, heavy skillet over medium-high heat. Cook, stirring constantly, about 2 to 5 minutes, until the spices start to look toasted and emit a wonderful aroma. Immediately place spices in a shallow bowl and let cool for 5 minutes. Place cooled spices in a spice/coffee grinder and grind until coarse.

3 Place dry-roasted spice mixture in a bowl and add salt, turmeric, garlic, and oil. Stir to form a paste.

4 Rub chicken with spice paste. Cover and refrigerate for 20 to 30 minutes.

5 Preheat oven to 350°F.

6 Arrange chicken in a single layer on a foil-lined baking pan. Roast about 25 minutes until chicken is tender.

Garlic and Pepper Chicken

[Serves 4]

 Tender pieces of chicken seasoned with garlic, ginger, and pepper. You can serve this dish on its own or use it to make Chicken Biriyani Rice (page 241).

1 pound boneless skinless chicken thighs*

3 tablespoons oil

2 or 3 curry leaves optional

3 or 4 (½- to 1-inch-long) slivers cinnamon stick

1 bay leaf

1 whole dried red chili pepper

½ teaspoon cumin seeds

½ teaspoon fennel seeds

½ cup chopped onions

4 garlic cloves peeled and cut in half

½ teaspoon ground turmeric

½ teaspoon salt

1 teaspoon Black Pepper and Cumin Powder (page 4)

2 teaspoons curry powder more, if desired

½ teaspoon garam masala

2 tablespoons minced fresh ginger

2 tablespoons tomato sauce

1 tablespoon chopped fresh cilantro

1 Cut chicken into small bite-size pieces. Set aside.

2 Heat oil in a skillet over medium heat. When oil is hot, but not smoking, add curry leaves, cinnamon sticks, bay leaf, red chili pepper, cumin seeds, and fennel seeds. Stir-fry until seeds turn light brown, about 30 seconds.

3 Add onions and garlic. Sauté for 1 to 2 minutes. Stir in turmeric.

4 Add chicken and salt to skillet. Cook, covered, over low heat until the chicken is browned.

5 Add Black Pepper and Cumin Powder, curry powder, and garam masala. Stir well to coat the chicken with spices. Add ginger and tomato sauce and stir. Stir in about ¼ cup of warm water to help prevent chicken from sticking to the bottom of the skillet.

6 Cover and cook over low to medium heat for 12 to 15 minutes, until chicken is tender. During the cooking process, check often and stir frequently to prevent chicken from sticking to the skillet.

7 Garnish with fresh cilantro.

*Boneless skinless chicken breasts may be used in place of chicken thighs, but more water (½ to 1 cup) will have to be added in Step 5 to maintain moistness. Adjust other seasonings according to taste.

Chicken Biriyani Rice I

[Serves 4 to 6]

 Biriyani is a highly aromatic and delicious basmati rice dish that can be either vegetarian or non-vegetarian. Chicken Biriyani Rice is essentially preparing "Garlic and Pepper Chicken" and cooking aromatic basmati rice seperately. Then combining both together to form a delicious symphony of flavors.

1 recipe Garlic and Pepper Chicken
   (page 239)

1 cup white basmati rice

3 tablespoons unsalted butter divided

2 or 3 slivers cinnamon sticks

1 bay leaf

¼ teaspoon cumin seeds

3 tablespoons grated fresh ginger

1 cup onion slices divided

¼ teaspoon ground turmeric

2 whole cloves

1 teaspoon ground cardamom

¼ teaspoon garam masala

3 saffron threads optional

1 teaspoon salt

2 cups chicken broth or hot water

¼ cup finely chopped cilantro

¼ cup roasted cashew halves

2 hard-boiled eggs dusted with ¼ teaspoon
   Black Pepper and Cumin Powder optional

1 Prepare "Garlic and Pepper Chicken," partially cooking the chicken. Set aside. (Note: For this recipe, you want to par-cook the chicken; par-cooking means just partially cooking it so that chicken can then finish cooking later in oven. This process allows the chicken to be moist and tender.)

2 Rinse rice in water 2 to 3 times to remove starch then soak rice in water for 5 minutes. Drain thoroughly. Set aside. Preheat oven to 350ºF.

3 Heat 2 tablespoons of butter in a large non-stick or stainless steel wide-bottomed saucepan over medium heat. Add cinnamon sticks, bay leaf, and cumin seeds and stir until light brown.

4 Add ginger and half of sliced onions. Sauté for 1 minute. Add rinsed basmati rice. Stir-fry rice for 2 to 3 minutes until slightly toasted.

5 Add turmeric, whole cloves, cardamom, garam masala, saffron (if using), salt, and 2 cups chicken broth or hot water. Stir together and bring to a boil.

6 Reduce to a simmer, cover, and continue cooking over low heat about 5 to 7 minutes, until all liquid is absorbed and rice is fluffy and tender.

7 Add reserved par-cooked "Garlic and Pepper Chicken" and stir gently to mix rice and chicken.

8 To complete the biriyani rice, transfer the rice with chicken into a rectangular baking dish (about 11 x 15 x 2 inches). Sprinkle top with remaining 1 tablespoon butter, remaining sliced onions, cilantro, and cashew halves. Cover the dish with aluminum foil. Place in a pre-heated oven and bake for about 15 to 20 minutes to cook through and maximize the aromatic flavor of rice with chicken.

9 Garnish with hard-boiled eggs and serve hot with Chicken Kurma (page 233).

Chicken Biriyani Rice II

[Serves 4]

 Biriyani is a highly aromatic and elaborate basmati rice dish that can be either vegetarian or non-vegetarian. This is a chicken-kurma-based biriyani rice. The recipe results in a more moist and flavorful biriyani rice!

1 recipe **Chicken Kurma** (page 233)

1 cup **basmati rice**

2 tablespoons **unsalted butter**

2 or 3 (½-inch-long) slivers **cinnamon stick**

1 **bay leaf**

2 to 4 **curry leaves** optional

1 cup **onion slices** cut lengthwise

½ teaspoon **garam masala**

2 whole **cloves**

½ teaspoon **ground cardamom**

2 tablespoons **minced fresh ginger**

1 tablespoon **fresh lemon juice**

1 teaspoon **salt**

¼ cup **chopped fresh cilantro**

½ cup **red onion slices** cut lengthwise

½ cup **roasted cashew pieces**

2 **hard-boiled eggs** dusted with ¼ teaspoon **Black Pepper and Cumin Powder**

1 Prepare Chicken Kurma and set aside. Preheat oven to 350ºF.

2 Cook rice in rice cooker or on stovetop (see page 79). Transfer cooked rice to a bowl, fluff the rice gently so the grains are separated. Set aside.

3 Melt butter in a large nonstick, wide-bottomed saucepan over medium heat. Add cinnamon sticks, bay leaf, and curry leaves and fry for about 30 seconds. Add onion slices and stir-fry for a few minutes. Immediately add the garam masala and cooked rice and stir gently into seasonings.

4 Add about 1 cup of the Chicken Kurma sauce to the rice and fluff the rice. Add half of the chicken pieces from the kurma sauce (or more chicken as desired). If more sauce is needed to coat the chicken add another ½ cup sauce.

5 Add cloves, cardamom, ginger, lemon juice, and salt. Mix with the rice and chicken.

6 Transfer the rice and chicken mixture into a rectangular baking dish. Cover the dish with aluminum foil. Bake in preheated oven for about 15 minutes to heat through and maximize the aromatic flavor.

7 Garnish with cilantro, red onion slices, and cashews. Place hard-boiled eggs over cooked biriyani rice when serving.

Turkey Meatballs

[Serves 4 to 5 / Makes 14 meatballs]

 These oven-baked meatballs are tasty, easy, and quick to prepare. You can also make them with ground chicken or lamb.

½ **pound ground turkey**

¼ **cup finely minced onion**

1 **teaspoon minced garlic cloves**

1½ **teaspoons ground turmeric**

1½ **teaspoons garam masala**

¼ **teaspoon salt**

¼ **teaspoon cayenne pepper powder** more or less to taste

1 **tablespoon minced fresh cilantro**

1 Preheat oven to 400°F.

2 Combine turkey, onion, garlic, turmeric, garam masala, salt, cayenne, and cilantro in a bowl. Mix well using your hands to ensure everything is evenly distributed.

3 Take 1 tablespoon of the turkey mixture into your hands and roll into a ball. Continue until you have used all of the mixture. You should have about 14 meatballs.

4 Place meatballs on a foil-lined baking sheet. Spray them on all sides with oil or cooking spray. Bake about 10 to 12 minutes, turning balls until browned and cooked through.

Ground Turkey Podimas with Split Peas and Coconut

[Serves 4]

 Delicately seasoned ground turkey makes a wonderful side dish! In the Chettinad region, Mutton Podimas are made by using ground lamb or goat meat, but I have found that ground turkey makes a delicious, healthy substitute. You can also use this mixture in a taco and add your favorite toppings.

½ cup yellow split peas or **moong dal (split yellow mung beans)**

½ teaspoon **ground turmeric** divided

2 tablespoons **oil**

1 dried **bay leaf**

2 to 4 (½-inch-long) slivers **cinnamon sticks**

½ teaspoon **cumin seeds**

½ teaspoon **fennel seeds**

½ cup **chopped onions**

2 to 4 **garlic cloves** finely chopped

1 fresh **green chili pepper** chopped (more, if desired)

½ pound **ground turkey**

1 teaspoon **curry powder**

½ teaspoon **cayenne pepper powder**

½ teaspoon **salt**

2 tablespoons **grated fresh coconut** or **unsweetened shredded coconut**

1 Bring 2 cups of water to a boil in a saucepan. Add split peas or moong dal and ¼ teaspoon turmeric. Reduce heat to medium and cook, uncovered, about 15 to 20 minutes, until split peas are tender and water is absorbed. (Add an additional ½ cup of water, if water is absorbed before split peas are tender.) Drain any remaining water and set aside.

2 Heat oil in a skillet over medium heat. When oil is hot, but not smoking, crumble bay leaf and cinnamon sticks into oil. Add cumin seeds and fennel seeds. Immediately add onions, garlic, chili pepper, and the remaining ¼ teaspoon turmeric. Cook, stirring, for about 1 minute, until onions are tender.

3 Add ground turkey. Fry for about 3 minutes until browned, stirring and breaking up meat as it cooks.

4 Stir in curry powder and cayenne. Cover and cook 2 minutes. Stir in salt, cover, and cook another 3 minutes.

5 Stir in cooked split peas or moong dal. Cover and cook another 2 minutes. Add coconut and stir well. Taste and add additional seasonings if desired.

Note: If the turkey becomes dry during the cooking process, beat one egg with a pinch of ground turmeric. Add the beaten egg to the turkey mixture and stir until egg is cooked. This process will moisten the resulting dish.

Lamb Kulambu

[Serves 4]

 There is nothing heartier than a lamb stew, and this one with its rich ginger-garlic sauce makes for a delicious satisfying meal.

1 pound lamb chops or leg of lamb

2 tablespoons oil

2 to 4 curry leaves optional

1 bay leaf

3 (½-inch-long) slivers cinnamon stick

¼ teaspoon fenugreek seeds

½ teaspoon cumin seeds

½ teaspoon fennel seeds

½ cup chopped onions

½ cup chopped tomatoes

3 garlic cloves quartered

2 tablespoons grated fresh ginger

½ teaspoon ground turmeric

2 teaspoons curry powder

½ teaspoon Black Pepper and Cumin Powder (page 4)

½ teaspoon cayenne pepper powder more or less to taste

½ cup tomato sauce

½ teaspoon salt more or less to taste

¼ cup chopped fresh cilantro

1 Remove fat from lamb and cut into small pieces as if for stew (you should have about 2 cups). Wipe the meat with a paper towel and reserve.

2 Heat oil in a skillet over medium-high heat. When the oil is hot but not smoking, add curry leaves, if using, bay leaf, cinnamon sticks, fenugreek seeds, cumin seeds, and fennel seeds. Stir until cumin seeds change color from light brown to semi-dark brown, about 30 seconds.

3 Add onions, tomatoes, garlic, ginger, and turmeric. Cook and stir for 2 to 3 minutes until onions are tender.

4 Add reserved lamb; cook and stir about 3 to 5 minutes until lamb begins to turn pink. Add curry powder, Black Pepper and Cumin Powder, and cayenne; stir to combine.

5 Add tomato sauce, 2 cups of warm water, salt, and cilantro and bring to a boil. Reduce heat to medium-low, cover, and simmer about 30 minutes, stirring occasionally and adding ¼ cup of water at a time, if needed, until lamb is tender and sauce thickens.

VARIATION

Lamb Saag can be prepared by adding **5 to 6 ounces fresh baby spinach** at the end of the recipe; when the lamb is tender stir the spinach into the saucy lamb dish and cook until it wilts.

Fish in Ginger Garlic Sauce

[Serves 4]

 Most types of fish lend themselves to Indian spices. Here the flavors of garlic, chili pepper, ginger, and a range of spices make this fish irresistible. This dish is quite easy to prepare and is a Chettinad specialty. The best fish to buy for this recipe are tilapia, cod, halibut, haddock, or white fish. Have the fishmonger cut into fillets if you desire.

3 tablespoons oil

2 to 4 curry leaves optional

½ teaspoon fenugreek seeds

½ teaspoon fennel seeds

½ teaspoon cumin seeds

1 cup chopped onions

¼ cup whole garlic cloves

1 fresh green chili pepper cut in half
lengthwise

¼ cup chopped tomatoes

½ teaspoon ground turmeric

2 teaspoons curry powder

1 teaspoon Black Pepper and Cumin Powder
(page 4)

1 teaspoon salt

2 cups tomato sauce

2 tablespoons minced fresh ginger

¼ teaspoon tamarind paste

1 pound firm-fleshed fish fillet cut into 4
(4-oz.) fillets

½ cup chopped fresh cilantro leaves

1 Place oil in a large saucepan over medium heat. When oil is hot, but not smoking, add curry leaves, fenugreek seeds, fennel seeds, and cumin seeds. Stir-fry until seeds are browned, about 30 seconds.

2 Add onions, garlic, chili pepper, and tomatoes. Stir-fry for about 1 minute. Stir in turmeric and cook for another minute. Add curry powder, Black Pepper and Cumin Powder, and salt. Stir and cook for another minute.

3 Add tomato sauce, ginger, and tamarind paste. Stir well into mixture. Add about 1 cup of warm water and stir well. Allow mixture to simmer, uncovered, for a few minutes over medium-low heat.

4 When mixture begins to boil, add fish fillets and spoon sauce carefully over fish. Add cilantro. Continue cooking over low heat, covered, for 5 to 7 minutes until fish is opaque and flaky. (Note: Sauce should be stirred gently during the cooking process; use the handles of the saucepan to swirl the sauce, rather than risk breaking the fish fillets with a spoon.)

5 When fish is cooked, remove saucepan from heat. Cover and let it remain at room temperature until serving. If fish is not served immediately, reheat only briefly before serving.

Spice-Rubbed Seared Fish

[Serves 4]

 A spice rub of cayenne, cumin, garlic, ginger, and lemon juice adds robust flavor to this easy, pan-seared fish recipe.

1 pound boneless skinless fish fillets (about 4 ounces each; use any firm fish such as salmon, halibut, tilapia, striped bass, catfish, haddock, or whitefish)

¾ teaspoon ground turmeric

½ teaspoon cayenne pepper powder more or less to taste

1 teaspoon ground cumin

½ teaspoon ground black pepper

½ teaspoon salt more or less to taste

1 tablespoon finely minced garlic cloves

1 tablespoon finely minced fresh ginger

1 teaspoon fresh lemon juice

2 to 4 chopped curry leaves optional

2 tablespoons oil

Chopped fresh cilantro for garnish

1 Dry fish with paper towels.

2 Mix turmeric, cayenne, cumin, black pepper, salt, garlic, ginger, lemon juice, and curry leaves, if using, together in a bowl.

3 Rub the spice mixture all over the fish fillets. Cover and marinate in the refrigerator for 20 to 30 minutes.

4 Heat oil in a skillet over medium-high heat. When the oil is hot but not smoking, add the fish fillets to the skillet. Make sure the pieces do not touch or they will steam and not brown. Pan-sear the fish until golden brown, about 3 to 5 minutes per side. Once cooked, place them on paper towels to absorb any excess oil.

5 Meanwhile, heat a plate for serving the fish. If your dishes are microwave-safe, microwaving them on high for a minute will work. Serve fish on the warm plate garnished with cilantro.

Salmon and Quinoa Patties

[Serves 4]

 Salmon is a popular fish choice these days. This recipe provides an interesting and flavorful alternative to the usual broiled salmon fillet. These patties are quick and easy to prepare, and a great way to boost your intake of omega-3s. Serve with Cilantro Chutney (page 39).

½ **cup dry quinoa**

½ **cup hot water**

8 **ounces wild salmon** skin removed

2 **handfuls fresh cilantro**

1 **teaspoon grated fresh ginger**

¼ **teaspoon Black Pepper and Cumin Powder** (page 4)

½ **teaspoon garam masala**

⅛ **teaspoon salt** more or less to taste

1 Prepare quinoa with ½ cup hot water as directed on page 79.

2 Cut salmon into ¼-inch square pieces; reserve.

3 Place cilantro in food processor and pulse until chopped. Add cooked quinoa, cubed salmon, ginger, Black Pepper and Cumin Powder, garam masala, and salt. Pulse several times until coarsely chopped. Do not over process—it should not be smooth.

4 Form salmon mixture into 4 patties and brush each with oil.

5 Heat skillet or grill pan over medium-high heat. Add patties and cook about 2 to 3 minutes per side or until golden brown.

6 Serve patties with Cilantro Chutney if desired.

Spicy Seared Shrimp

[Serves 4]

 Also known as "Shrimp Masala," this recipe sears shrimp with ginger, garlic, and enticing spices. Serve the shrimp over rice, quinoa, or polenta with vegetables for a flavorful, fulfilling meal!

1 pound (10 to 12) fresh raw medium or
   large shrimp*

2 tablespoons oil

¼ teaspoon cumin seeds

¼ cup finely chopped onions

2 tablespoons finely chopped tomatoes

1 tablespoon minced garlic cloves

1 tablespoon minced fresh ginger

¼ teaspoon ground turmeric

1 teaspoon curry powder

1 teaspoon Black Pepper and Cumin Powder
   (page 4)

2 to 3 tablespoons tomato sauce

½ teaspoon salt more or less to taste

2 tablespoons minced cilantro

1 Peel and devein the shrimp. (To devein, make a shallow cut lengthwise down the outer curve of the shrimp's body and remove the dark ribbon-like string.) Rinse, pat dry with paper towels, and reserve.*

2 Heat oil in a skillet over medium-high heat. When the oil is hot but not smoking, add the cumin seeds and stir until cumin seeds change color from light brown to semi-dark brown, about 30 seconds.

3 Add onions, tomatoes, garlic, ginger, and turmeric. Cook 2 to 3 minutes while stirring, until onion is translucent. Stir in curry powder, Black Pepper and Cumin Powder, tomato sauce, and salt.

4 Add shrimp and sauté about 2 to 3 minutes until flesh changes from gray translucent to pink. (Do not overcook as shrimp toughen quickly.)

5 Garnish with cilantro and serve warm.

*Peeled and deveined shrimp are also readily available in the frozen section; simply thaw the shrimp, pat dry and skip Step 1.

Shrimp in Eggplant Sauce

[Serves 4]

 Shrimp and eggplant make a unique and enticing combination of flavors and textures in this creative dish.

2 tablespoons oil

2 to 4 curry leaves optional

½ teaspoon cumin seeds

½ cup chopped onions

½ cup chopped tomatoes

¼ teaspoon ground turmeric

2 cups cubed unpeeled eggplant

1 teaspoon cayenne pepper powder more, if
  desired

1 teaspoon ground cumin

1 cup tomato sauce

¼ teaspoon tamarind paste

1 teaspoon salt

½ pound (about 15) fresh or frozen shrimp
  peeled and deveined

1 Heat oil in a saucepan over medium heat. When oil is hot, but not smoking, add curry leaves and cumin seeds. Immediately add onions, tomatoes, and turmeric and cook for a few minutes.

2 Add eggplant and allow to cook with the seasonings for a few minutes.

3 Stir in cayenne and ground cumin. Add tomato sauce, tamarind paste, salt, and 1½ cups of warm water. Let eggplant cook over low heat, covered, until soft and sauce has thickened.

4 When the eggplant is cooked and the mixture begins to thicken, add the shrimp. Cook for about 5 minutes. If the sauce is too thick, add an additional ½ cup to 1 cup of warm water and let it simmer for a few additional minutes.